Do it as if
your life depends
-on it, 8/13/22

THE
EDUCATION
OF A
VALUE
INVESTOR

THE
EDUCATION
OF A
VALUE
INVESTOR

My Transformative Quest for Wealth,
Wisdom, and Enlightenment

Guy Spier

St. Martin's Press

New York

www.stmartins.com

Designed by Letra Libre, Inc.

Library of Congress Cataloging-in-Publication Data

Spier, Guy.
    The education of a value investor / Guy Spier.
        p.   cm.
    ISBN 978-1-137-27881-4 (hardcover)
    1. Spier, Guy. 2. Investment advisors—United States—Biography. 3. Investment bankers—United States—Biography. 4. Investments. I. Title.
    HG4928.5.S65A3   2014
    332.6092—dc23
    [B]

                                                                2014010919

Our books may be purchased in bulk for promotional, educational, or business use. Please contact your local bookseller or the Macmillan Corporate and Premium Sales Department at 1-800-221-7945, extension 5442, or by e-mail at MacmillanSpecialMarkets@macmillan.com.

First published by Palgrave Macmillan, a division of St. Martin's Press LLC

First edition: September 2014

20   19   18   17   16   15

To my parents, Marilyn and Simon Spier, and to my sister, Tanya.

To my children, Eva, Isaac, and Sarah.

To my wife, Lory:

You are all my reasons.

CONTENTS

INTRODUCTION

MY GOAL IN WRITING THIS BOOK IS TO SHARE SOME OF what I've learned on my path as an investor. It's about the education of *this* investor, not any other investor. This story is not an investment how-to. It's not a road map. Rather, it's the story of my journey and of what I've learned along the way. With my own flaws and foibles and idiosyncratic abilities—and despite my considerable blind spots.

Over the years, I've stumbled across some profound insights and powerful tools that I'd like to share with you. In most cases, these are not things that are written about in textbooks. Because it's a story about how things happen in the real world—and because the real world is messy—the topics are broad in scope. They range from the most insignificant of habits that I've developed, like what to read first, to the grandest: whom to choose as heroes and mentors and how their wisdom can change your life.

This book traces the arc of a transformation. I started off as a Gordon Gekko wannabe—brash, shortsighted, and entirely out for myself. Then a series of transformations and self-realizations led me on a path from Benjamin Graham's *The Intelligent Investor* to Ruane Cunniff to *Poor Charlie's Almanack* to Robert Cialdini, then to meeting Mohnish Pabrai and lunch with Warren Buffett. That $650,100 meal had a life-changing impact on me, as you will see.

Within one year of my meeting with Buffett, I let two-thirds of my staff in New York go, stashed half of my family's belongings in storage, and shipped the other half to Zurich, where we went to live.

I stopped charging management fees to new investors in my funds. I switched off my Bloomberg monitor. And I renounced my perilous addiction to checking stock prices on a minute-by-minute basis.

I'm not necessarily advocating that you should also have lunch with Warren Buffett—especially now that the price tag has soared, hitting a high of $3.46 million in 2012! And I'm not claiming to have a special understanding of him either. What I *can* tell you is that he has had an extraordinary impact on how I invest and on the way I live my life. My hope is that I can share some of these lessons that I've derived from him so that they will benefit you as much as they have benefited me.

It took me the best part of two decades to get onto a more enlightened path in life, and I've made many missteps and lost much time along the way. Hopefully, this book will help you to reach your enlightened path faster, and with fewer missteps. As Buffett once said, "Try to learn from your mistakes—better yet, learn from the mistakes of others!"

I submit to you that if you learn only some of the lessons here, you cannot help but become rich—and perhaps wildly rich. Certainly, the wisdom I've gleaned—not just from my heroes, but from my own mistakes and successes—has helped me immeasurably as an investor. As I write this, I've had a cumulative return of 463 percent since founding the Aquamarine Fund in 1997, versus 167 percent for the S&P 500 index. In other words, $1 million invested in the fund would now be worth $5.63 million, versus $2.7 million if it had been invested in the S&P 500.

But this book is also about the inner game of investing, and by extension, the inner game of life. As I've come to discover, investing is about much more than money. So as your wealth grows, I hope you will also come to realize that the money is largely irrelevant. And what you will want to do with the bulk of your wealth is give it back to society.

You're not quite sure about that last part? That's okay. For much of my life, I wasn't sure about it myself, and a part of me still doubts it. Like you, I'm a work in progress.

We're told a lot these days about why capitalism has failed us. We're told that greedy bankers and irresponsible CEOs need to be reined in with more stringent regulations, and that wealth should be more aggressively redistributed. Perhaps. But greed can also be a vehicle to something deeper and more soulful. In my experience, you can start out as a hungry young capitalist, driven almost entirely by greed, and find that it gradually leads you to a more enlightened mind-set. In that case, greed may be good after all—not if it merely motivates you to acquire more, but if it drives you toward that inner journey of spiritual growth and enlightenment.

I expand on that lesson at the very end. But first, let's enter the belly of the beast.

1

FROM THE BELLY OF THE BEAST TO WARREN BUFFETT

O that this too too sullied flesh would melt,
Thaw and resolve itself into a dew!

. . .

How weary, stale, flat, and unprofitable,
Seem to me all the uses of this world!
Fie on't! ah fie! 'tis an unweeded garden,
That grows to seed; things rank and gross in nature
Possess it merely.
—Hamlet, act 1, scene 2, lines 129–130
and 133–137

HAVE YOU EVER FELT THAT WAY? UTTER SELF-loathing. Unlike Hamlet, at least I wasn't suicidal. But I felt almost as wretched. I was disgusted with investment bankers as a breed, and especially the ones I worked with. I felt the same way about my investment banking firm. Worst of all, though, I was disgusted with myself.

Less than two years earlier, I had felt ready to conquer the world. Back then, I was a student at Harvard Business School (HBS). For good measure, I also had a degree from Oxford University, where I'd come top of my class in economics. Everything had seemed possible—until I threw it all away with one recklessly foolish career move.

In 1993, a few months before I graduated from Harvard, I stumbled upon a job listing for an assistant to the chairman at D. H. Blair Investment Banking Corp. I'd read a bit about investment banking and fancied myself as one of these budding Masters of the Universe.

Brimming with youthful confidence, I headed to New York City to meet with D. H. Blair's chairman, J. Morton Davis. Morty had started out as a poor Jewish kid from Brooklyn. He graduated from Harvard Business School in 1959 and went on to become the owner and chairman of D. H. Blair, which had been founded in 1904. People told me that he'd made hundreds of millions for himself.

I met with him in his wood-paneled corner office at 44 Wall Street. The place hadn't been renovated in years, and it looked like a traditional investment banking partnership from John Pierpont Morgan's era. In fact, J. P. Morgan's headquarters were almost next door.

Morty was a consummate salesman, and he did a brilliant job of beguiling me. He talked to me about some of the great deals he'd pulled off in hot areas like biotech, adding, "You'll be doing deals right away, working directly with me." He assured me that there was "no limit" to what I could achieve there with him and later gave me a book by Frank Bettger called *How I Raised Myself from Failure to Success in Selling*. I liked the fact that Morty was an outsider—unconventional, self-made, and highly successful.

Shortly afterward, I read a *New York Times* article that referred to D. H. Blair as an "infamous" brokerage house whose "brokers have been known to refuse to let customers sell when they request that a stock be liquidated." The article also mentioned that securities regulators in Delaware had "tried to revoke Blair's license" and that regulators in Hawaii "said Blair was using fraudulent and deceptive sales practices." When I went back to ask him about the article, Morty told me that people envy success and try to take you down. I was gullible enough to believe whatever he told me.

Some of my friends from Harvard raised their eyebrows when they heard that I was going to work for D. H. Blair, but I ignored their warnings. I was arrogant and slightly rebellious, and I was determined not to follow the standard route to establishment firms like Goldman Sachs and J. P. Morgan. I wanted to blaze my own trail and be more entrepreneurial. It felt as if Morty had made me an offer that I couldn't refuse, although I should have. So I signed on, thinking that I was golden, expecting Wall Street to show me the money.

High on hope, I joined D. H. Blair in September 1993 with the grand title of vice president. I shared a dimly lit, wood-paneled room on the second floor with a kind, elderly banker. He hadn't done a deal in years, but he was part of the scenery, burnishing the investment bank's sheen of respectability.

Only six months into the job, I was miserable. I had received and continued to receive a series of hard knocks. For a start, I had thought that I'd be the chairman's sole assistant and that I'd have the opportunity to observe and learn from the master by helping him analyze the multitude of opportunities coming his way. Instead, it turned out that he had two other assistants.

All three of us had shiny new MBAs: Len had gone to Harvard Business School; Drew was from Wharton. This was a dog-eat-dog environment, and the three of us were not a team. As I soon realized, there was absolutely no need for me on the analysis front. I was learning the hard way about what is normal on Wall Street. There are always more people available, and they are abundantly capable of doing the job that needs to be done. The competition is intense. And there are dozens of people lined up right behind you, ready to take your place.

The only way I could add any value in this environment, and what the firm really needed me to do, was to bring in deals. I thought that I was up to the challenge. After all, it was a big selling point of the job. But the competition was fierce, both inside and outside the firm. And I was new. New to D. H. Blair, new to investment banking and finance, and new to New York.

I was determined not to quit, though. That would have been an admission of defeat. I would have been mortified to let my classmates know that I'd made a mistake. Even worse, I would have been called a quitter, and that reputation might have followed me. More than anything, what motivated me was how other people viewed me rather than how I viewed myself. If this had been reversed, I don't think I would have stuck around that place for a minute; I would have simply ditched. But I was desperate to look successful.

My singular goal became to get a deal done. That way, I could declare victory and then choose to leave. So I smiled and dialed and pounded the pavement for many months, following up on every deal lead I possibly could. But I still came up empty-handed. Despite my massive testosterone-fueled determination to succeed in this, my first job after graduating with an MBA, I was hopelessly flailing.

My problem wasn't just that the best deals got nabbed by the big names like Goldman Sachs and Morgan Stanley, although that was true. There were plenty of other opportunities around. But successfully bringing those deals into D. H. Blair required me to do things with facts that I had never done.

D. H. Blair's specialty was venture capital and banking. It was one of the things that had attracted me to the firm: the opportunity to be on the cutting edge, funding start-ups with new technologies that would change the world. Oh, and did I mention that I would also get filthy rich in the process? In addition to my arrogance and hubris, I also had my fair share of Wall Street greed. I was convinced that I was on the quick path to Nirvana.

The harsh reality was that companies with technologies or innovations that really worked and were certain to succeed were extremely rare—even among the crowd that got its funding from more prominent investment banks like Goldman Sachs and Morgan Stanley.

Instead, the vast majority fell into the category of "might succeed." There were a great many management teams that desperately wanted to pursue their dreams and that were willing to do and say pretty much anything if it meant getting funding. Before I knew it, I was drowning in a sea of crappy deals, assailed by entrepreneurs who hoped that I would look kindly upon them.

The inexorable logic of expected probability that I had first learned about in high school and then studied at Harvard in a course called "Decision Theory" was that if I was going to recommend a deal, it had to have at least a fair chance of making money. Given how many deals failed, and the very small number that made investors a multiple of their original investment, my rough calculation was that the probability of success had to be at least 50 percent for the thing to get funded. But after a while, I came to believe that D. H. Blair's standards were far lower.

On one memorable occasion I was called into a meeting between the bank and an outfit looking to raise money for a cold fusion venture. Having studied the materials and read up a little on the background, I blurted out, "But the science just doesn't make sense!"

Implicitly, what I meant was, "Do you really expect me to keep a straight face and tell our salespeople that this crap is going to fly?"

In another example, our firm IPO'd a company that was going to build a new space station—in conjunction with the Baikonur Cosmodrome in Kazakhstan—based on contracts with companies and entities formed by ex-government officials of this former Soviet republic. The company's only assets seemed to be sketchy contracts written in a foreign language that were unlikely to be enforceable in a Kazakh court, let alone in New York or London. Like the cold fusion nonsense, the probability that this thing would take flight was pretty low.

But this was the business of D. H. Blair: find some of the more extraordinary outlier opportunities, then hawk them to a naïve and hopeful investing public that knew no better.

To be fair, even though many of these "opportunities" turned out to be duds and eventually failed, the firm also scored a big hit every now and then. For example, it had taken public one of the first biotech companies, Enzo Biochem, at a time when it was unthinkable to do an IPO for a company without earnings. And from time to time, D. H. Blair even IPO'd businesses that generated real and growing earnings. But in between the good deals, the firm needed fodder to feed the money-making machine.

On the deal side, in addition to cash investment banking fees, D. H. Blair would take a healthy chunk of warrants in the companies that it financed. And on the investment side, D. H. Blair was often the only market maker in the shares that it took public. With bid-ask spreads as high as 20 percent, there were fat profits to be made just buying and selling the companies that went public. Like so many institutions on Wall Street, D. H. Blair had a nice edge on its clients.

But generating trading volume in the stocks and getting a broader group of people interested in them required a lot of stage management. Dressing up an opportunity with questionable odds of success and turning it into something that the public was enthusiastic about buying was part of the role of D. H. Blair's analysts and investment bankers. To make one of these deals succeed and to grease the wheels of finance, various people needed to play their part.

The cold fusion and Cosmodrome deals were not going to earn any money soon, if ever. But they did have sizzle. These companies represented ideas that could capture the public's imagination. If an enthusiastic investing public ended up developing a mania for cold fusion or space stations, this could easily propel the newly IPO'd stock into the stratosphere, to many multiples of its IPO price. From an investment banking standpoint, this sort of price action would make the deal a runaway success—even if the company eventually failed. As the stock rose, the bank would cash in on the warrants and make a profit trading the shares. If the company ultimately went bust, the shares would be broadly held, and it would not be D. H. Blair or its clients that bore the brunt of the loss.

To get these sorts of situations going required aggressive salesmanship of every kind. So D. H. Blair had a retail brokerage unit filled with hard-charging brokers who called clients from a boiler room on the 14th floor. They were physically and legally separated from the investment bankers like me, and they officially worked for another company. While they were part of D. H. Blair & Co., I was employed by D. H. Blair Investment Banking Corp.

Our tiny team of bankers constituted the acceptable, respectable face of the company, while the brokers were the backroom boys, touting these dubious deals to unsophisticated retail investors. They were chillingly reminiscent of the brokers in Martin Scorsese's movie *The Wolf of Wall Street,* which was exaggerated but not misleading. The 14th floor of D. H. Blair was a swirling sea of testosterone; someone once told me that hookers would sometimes go up there to reward the most successful salesman of the day.

I had no direct dealings with these guys, but they depended on our investment banking team to come up with deals for them to tout. The bankers could live with themselves because they were holed up in the handsome, wood-paneled cocoon of the second floor, while the really eye-opening activities went on 12 floors above. Still, the brokers needed us bankers as enablers.

It was only after a year or so at D. H. Blair that it really started to dawn on me that this was a big part of the role I was expected to play. I was supposed to dress up the least sketchy of these deals in such a way that the downsides were heavily de-emphasized or ignored while the sizzle—the blue-sky upside—was highlighted.

I wasn't there to act as a careful, well-trained analyst. They had no use for a forensic arbiter who painstakingly researched an idea, examined the opportunity, and pronounced, as accurately and honestly as possible, what this thing really was. In hindsight, I can see with clarity that the real value to the firm of my Oxford degree and my Harvard MBA was to adorn its deals and documents with my pristine credentials. I thereby provided a kind of Ivy League fig leaf.

When I look back to our meeting with the cold fusion company, I can see how naïve I was. In truth, everyone there was expecting me to play my part. The elephant in the room was an unspoken dialogue that went something like this:

COLD FUSION COMPANY MANAGEMENT: Execs of D. H. Blair, yes, we are bullshitting you. This is almost certainly not going to work, but we've been working on it for years and have invested substantial personal funds in it. In any case, nobody can prove 100 percent that it *won't* work. Moreover, think of the excitement that this thing will cause among investors and the press. It would be the only publicly traded nuclear fusion power company in the world!

OTHER D. H. BLAIR INVESTMENT BANKERS: Yes, this is extremely unlikely to fly, but we need to fill our pipeline of deals so that you, the company management, can get rich on the founder stock and we, the investment bank, can get rich on fees and from trading the stock. And who knows, it might even succeed, in which case our clients might even make money too.

In the midst of this cynical ritual, I was oblivious enough to mention that the physics was apparently bogus, remarking, "There are so many people out there who've claimed that they have made cold fusion work, and there's nothing new here." I was so tactless that I actually laughed out loud.

Only in retrospect did I realize that I had instantly become the most hated person in that room. How could this deal ever fly if nitwits like me couldn't keep their big mouths shut? There was no way I was going to succeed in this environment with that kind of reckless honesty.

But I didn't want to concede defeat. So I doubled down on my efforts, girding myself for more toil and trouble. I smiled some more and dialed some more. And I pounded many more pavements.

Eventually, I found a deal with far better chances than most. This time, I could put my hand on my heart and say that, in spite of the risks, it deserved to get funding. The company was called Telechips, and in 1994 it had a communications device that was both a computer and a telephone. The management team was led by C. A. ("Al") Burns, formerly at Bell Labs, and Randy Pinato, a former salesman for one of the Baby Bells. The idea was solid, although well before its time. This was before the commercialization of the Internet, and cell phones had only recently been introduced.

I had also found an experienced investment banker, Howard Phillips, who was willing to work with me in structuring the deal and raising the funding. Phillips had a solid background at Oppenheimer and had come to D. H. Blair in semiretirement. He worked in the office two or three days a week, and he had taken a mild liking to me.

But having found a solid management team and convinced them that Phillips and I were their path to funding, I discovered a whole new realm of pain and unpleasantness. In spite of my understanding that Phillips and I were equal partners, I soon discovered that our fee split for doing the deal wasn't going to be 50–50, after all. He was taking the lion's share. I felt the hit to my pride more keenly than the one to my pocketbook. Still, if the deal was going to get done, I had no choice but to accept this.

The next step was to get the deal approved. I imagined that, given some of the dreck I'd seen in my short time there, this more plausible deal would just sail through. Phillips and I went through the investment committee and got a letter of intent stating the valuation and the amount we would raise for Telechips, subject to some cursory due-diligence checks. I was ecstatic.

So were Al and Randy, and we celebrated. They were elated that they could stop exhausting themselves in their pursuit of funding and could focus instead on building their business. Randy told me they had also been working on a highly credible alternative source of funding, but they were delighted to be working with me because they liked me.

For my part, I was already pre-spending some of my (smaller) bonus and thinking of how I'd report this news to Class Notes, a Harvard alumni newsletter. Something along the lines of "Guy Spier does his first deal within 18 months of leaving HBS."

Howard Phillips, an old hand at this game, had not pre-spent any of his (much larger) portion of our expected bonus bonanza. He must have understood that the cursory due-diligence checks were nothing of the sort. Our chairman, Morty Davis, had assigned this task to one of the other young investment bankers, who then proceeded to nitpick the deal to death. I couldn't believe it. He had been perfectly happy to cheerlead many other, much worse deals.

Eventually, with Telechips management wondering what the holdup was, and with me at a loss for answers, we were all summoned to another meeting. By now, the Telechips team was desperate for funding as the company was burning through cash. I learned that because of the nitpicks (sorry, I mean serious due diligence), the deal could still get done, but at a far lower valuation than our original term sheet had promised—and with much heftier fees now payable to the investment bank.

I got a call from Randy, telling me how appalled he was by the bank's behavior and with me for stringing them along. All I could do was apologize and say that I honestly hadn't known that it would turn out this way. I hoped he believed me, but I'm still not sure he did. On a personal level, I'd certainly lost his trust, not to mention his friendship.

A day or two later, Telechips accepted the term sheet—as everyone knew they would. They had been strung along until the investment committee was confident that the company would have no alternative. I was incensed and disgusted—not least with myself.

Looking back, I now realize that I was potentially teetering on the edge of a moral cliff. If I had been drawn any further into this firm's culture, either willingly or unwillingly, I would have fallen irretrievably off that cliff.

In fact, a few years after I left, D. H. Blair, having run afoul of the regulators, was reduced to a shadow of its former self. The retail brokerage business, D. H. Blair & Co., closed down entirely in 1998. In 2000, the *Wall Street Journal* reported that this retail brokerage unit and 15 of its officers and employees had been indicted on 173 counts of stock fraud.

Among other things, the retail brokerage firm was charged with manipulating stock prices for its own benefit and engaging in illegal sales tactics. Four executives at the retail firm—chairman Kenton Wood, vice chairmen Alan Stahler and Kalman Renov, and head trader Vito Capotorto—pleaded guilty to securities fraud and collusion to fix stock prices. *USA Today* reported that D. H. Blair & Co. and its executives paid $21 million "to reimburse defrauded customers."

The investment bank, which was a separate company, emerged unscathed—and no criminal charges were brought against its chairman, Morty Davis. But it must have been a terrible time for him, not least because Stahler and Renov were his sons-in-law. In the press, Morty himself took a beating. For example, a 1998 article in *Forbes* referred to "the controversial figure of penny-stock king, J. Morton Davis," who "got rich by raising money in the private and public markets for companies that tonier firms wouldn't touch." When I left Harvard and went to work on deals with him, this wasn't quite what I had in mind.

What's sad is that Morty truly wasn't a bad person. I remember going for a family dinner at his house one Friday evening and being touched by how kindly and warmly he included me. There was much to admire in him, and it's certainly not for me to judge anyone.

Still, from what I had seen of the culture at D. H. Blair, its problems with regulators were hardly surprising.

For my part, I don't know for sure how close I was to the edge of that moral cliff. But knowing what I know now, I can tell you that a thousand miles away would have been too close. In retrospect, I had been dangerously blind about the motives and ethics of my colleagues. This was powerful proof of just how dumb even smart, well-educated people can be.

It certainly took me far too long to grasp that this business was set up in such a way that, if I wanted to win, I would have to lose whatever was left of my moral compass. For months, I was focused on the wrong questions, wondering why I was having so much trouble getting deals done and fretting that something must be wrong with me. I didn't have the experience or the perspective to understand that this whole environment was wrong.

Part of the problem was that the competition was so fierce. This led to the belief that, if I wasn't willing to do something, someone else would quickly step in to do it. This kind of environment is perfectly designed to get people to push the boundaries in order to succeed. It's a pattern that's repeated again and again on Wall Street. Through ambition, greed, arrogance, or naïveté, many bright, hard-working people have strayed into gray areas.

Still, it's important to clarify one point. No member of D. H. Blair's management ever directly asked me to lie or misrepresent anything—even though I believed that a big aspect of the place was about misrepresenting opportunities to a credulous marketplace.

For example, they would have appreciated my claiming that I had done my due diligence on cold fusion and that it checked out. Bang! They would have had one piece of the ideal scenery they needed in order to close the deal. But they never said as much in so many words. The rules of the game were implicit.

At D. H. Blair, I observed another pattern that plays itself out countless times on Wall Street. Everybody wants to make money. So the senior greedy bankers who should know better turn a blind eye while the younger greedy, naïve bankers push the boundaries. At Lehman Brothers, they pushed leverage. At Countrywide, they ignored default rates on subprime. At SAC Capital, they turned a blind eye to rampant insider trading.

My experience at D. H. Blair has helped me to see how often this sort of thing recurs in a wide variety of environments on Wall Street. During the tech bubble of the late 1990s, lousy companies were talked up and sold to an unsuspecting public. For example, analysts like Henry Blodget at Merrill Lynch were wildly bullish about Internet stocks, dressing up pigs with lipstick. Years later, the same thing happened at credit-rating agencies where analysts issued blindly positive ratings for the CMOs and CDOs that would ultimately lead to the housing crisis.

As for me, my 18 gut-wrenching months at D. H. Blair had destroyed my clean copybook and brought my career to an absolute low. The résumé and reputation I had built for myself at Oxford and Harvard had been reduced to dust. And reputation in business—especially the investing world—is everything. For years after I left D. H. Blair, I felt so sullied by the experience that it was as if I couldn't wash the dirt off my hands.

Even as I write about this now, my skin crawls. Part of me wonders if it's a mistake to write about it at all. But I think it's important to discuss just how easy it is for any of us to get caught up in things that might seem unthinkable—to get sucked into the wrong environment and make moral compromises that can tarnish us terribly. We like to think that we change our environment, but the truth is that it changes us. So we have to be extraordinarily careful to choose the right environment—to work with, and even socialize with, the right people. Ideally, we should stick close to people who are better than us so that we can become more like them.

I hope the decision to work at D. H. Blair will turn out to be the worst mistake of my professional life. But, thankfully, it didn't break me. In an article entitled "Trauma Reveals the Roots of Resilience," the psychologist Diana Fosha quotes a line from Ernest Hemingway: "The world breaks everyone and afterward some are strong at the broken places." Why is it that some people are strengthened by their traumas and not broken by them?

It's a great question that can also be asked about business and investing. Warren Buffett made one of his bigger mistakes when, in his thirties, he invested in the loss-making Berkshire Hathaway textile mills. This could have been his undoing, but he later transformed Berkshire Hathaway into the towering monument of his life. He did so in part by learning to invest in better businesses instead of betting on the cigar-butt stocks (like Berkshire) that Ben Graham had taught him to buy. Perhaps D. H. Blair was my own cigar-butt move: a formative experience of toxic shock.

It's not just a quaint, self-help idea that the people who succeed are those who get up when life knocks them down. An essential component of our education is to learn from our mistakes—and if we don't make mistakes, sometimes we may not learn at all. Certainly, the whole D. H. Blair debacle was an essential component of my education as a value investor.

One of the biggest lessons was that I must never do anything again that could taint my reputation. As Buffett once warned, "It takes 20 years to build a reputation and five minutes to ruin it. If you think about that, you'll do things differently." Another lesson was that I had to do everything I could to change my professional and intellectual environment.

When I discovered the world of Warren Buffett, it was as if I had found a lifeline. The discovery happened one summer day around the time that the Telechips deal came across my desk. By then, I was already deeply disillusioned with the life I was leading. I found myself no longer eating sandwiches at my desk on the second floor at D. H. Blair. I'd lost my desire to build this sort of career, but I had no idea what to do and was afraid to leave for fear of seeming like a loser or a quitter.

Looking for an escape, I'd sneak out at lunchtime and buy a falafel or a *shawarma* from a street vendor. Then I'd wander into Zuccotti Park in the shadow of the World Trade Center and play a few games of pick-up chess.

On the way back, I'd often duck into a business bookshop on Broadway just off Wall Street and browse the shelves. The first book I bought there was Frank Fabozzi's *Bond Markets, Analysis and Strategies*. I was engrossed by his technical discussions of asset/liability matching and the measurement of bond duration. For a while, I even imagined myself as a bond trader.

On another visit to this store, I picked up Ben Graham's seminal book, *The Intelligent Investor,* featuring a preface by Buffett. I could not put it down. Graham spoke eloquently of owning a stock not as a piece of paper to trade, but as a share in a real business. He also talked of treating "Mr. Market" like a manic depressive and taking advantage of his shifting moods. As the market veers between fear and greed, investors can profit richly by focusing in a clearheaded way on the intrinsic value of a company and exploiting the discrepancy between the price and the value. Sometimes you know in your bones that something is true. To me, this value-investing philosophy made so much sense that it was self-evident.

Before long, I also read *Buffett: The Making of an American Capitalist,* a brilliant biography by Roger Lowenstein. I was captivated by the details of Buffett's life. There could not have been a more flagrant contrast between the way he lived and the way I was living. And there could not have been a starker contrast between my deal-making experiences at D. H. Blair and his own business ethos. Buffett wasn't working in a snake pit. He wasn't finding pretexts to sell dubious dreck to hard-working folks on Main Street or hustling for a fatter share of brokerage fees and then stabbing his peers in the back.

I had no clue yet how to implement any of this in my own life. But I felt a deep and desperate need to get out of where I was and move closer to where he was. It was as if he were holding out his hand to me so that I could drag myself out of the moral quagmire in which I was sinking. I clung to him for dear life.

This book is about my journey from that dark place toward the Nirvana where I now live.

2

THE PERILS OF AN ELITE EDUCATION

IN ORDER TO MOVE FORWARD, I HAD TO FIX WHAT WAS broken. I had to figure out what was wrong with my wiring so that I could rewire myself. So I began to ask myself why I'd gone to D. H. Blair in the first place: what possessed a purportedly smart person to do something so spectacularly foolish? After all, there were many other options open to me. This exploration was the beginning of my inward journey. And one of the things I came to realize was that my ivory tower education had left me dangerously exposed and vulnerable.

My ending up at D. H. Blair was certainly a betrayal of the purposes of my education at Oxford and Harvard. I'd attended two of the world's finest institutions only to become an inadvertent accomplice in a perversion of the finance industry.

Did my education fail me? Or, even worse, did I fail my education? There's a larger question to be asked here, too, since I'm also a microcosm of my peer group. Why did so many highly educated people from elite business schools and privileged backgrounds contribute to and exacerbate the financial crisis of 2008–2009? Did our education fail us? Or did we fail our education? These questions haven't been answered adequately by the prestigious universities that groomed all these high-powered creators of economic mayhem.

I have to ask these questions even if I'm not qualified to answer them. Because what was going on in my life was, in many ways, just an extreme reflection of what was going on in the lives of my peers. So many of us went into finance with tremendous confidence in our intelligence and abilities, only to discover that the system we became part of was capable of causing more harm than good.

The unsettling truth is that there are elements of an elite education that are positively a disadvantage. I wasn't aware of these disadvantages at the time that I finished my formal education or for about a decade afterward. On some level, I had my eyes closed and was cruising on autopilot for quite a while, wasting what should have been some of the most productive years of my life. If you had an educational experience that was anything like mine, you—like me—may have to reprogram and rewire yourself in some fundamental ways.

The person who has influenced me most as an investor is Mohnish Pabrai, an Indian immigrant to the United States who has racked up far better returns than I have. He studied at Clemson University in South Carolina, not at Oxford or Harvard. And when Mohnish and I had our charity lunch with Warren Buffett, you can be sure that Warren (who had failed to gain admission to Harvard Business School) couldn't have cared less where either of us had studied.

Don't get me wrong. Places like Oxford and Harvard are wonderful, and I appreciate their immense contribution to our civilization. But in lionizing them, we can fail to discern their drawbacks. So if some of what I say about these universities sounds overly harsh, please understand that it's a harshness born of affection and a desire to build up, rather than tear down.

Part of the problem is that a finely trained but rarefied academic mind can be damaging to your long-term success. You can easily end up with the mental equivalent of a Formula 1 Ferrari, when what you need in the real world is a hardy Jeep that can operate adequately in a variety of environments.

To explain this, let me first give you some background on the particularities of my own formal education. I came to Oxford from the City of London Freemen's School—an independent high school originally founded for the benefit of orphans. Gullible parents imagined that it was a fancy English private school, but it was really a less-exalted crammer. Many of the educational decisions there were made on the basis of what would get the most students into the best universities. Some of the teachers were remarkable. But for the most part, the goal wasn't to educate us in a broad sense. Instead, it was merely to analyze what it would take for us to perform well in our A-Level and university entrance exams. The system then streamed and drilled us so we could get the highest scores.

My Oxford entrance papers consisted of Math, Physics, and a General Paper. And guess what? The system worked: I'd been so well trained that, despite disastrously misreading the instructions on one exam, I was accepted at Brasenose College, Oxford, to study law.

But now I was alongside students who had been more broadly educated and who knew stuff that I did not. Although I loved jurisprudence, or legal philosophy, the curriculum also required me to wade through dozens of British common-law cases each week. Now, British common law is a phenomenal subject. But not for an 18-year-old whose family had immigrated to the United Kingdom seven years earlier and who had little social or historical knowledge of the country. I started to have recurring dreams in which I could press a special button that would incinerate every tome of common law on the planet. I believe that it's never good to ignore your recurring dreams for long.

Contrast this experience with that of a friend at Brasenose, Andrew Feldman (now Lord Andrew Feldman, chairman of Britain's Conservative Party). He'd studied copious amounts of British and world history and was able to set the law within its current and historical social context. For Andrew, the law was a fascinating microcosm of everything he had already studied. For me, it was morass of intractable case law. I had been prepared to pass exams, but I didn't have the benefit of his broader framework. There's an important lesson here: It's not enough to be in a great program at a great school. You need to be in a program that matches your particular needs at that stage in your life. Back then, studying law was wrong for me.

It was in this state of dissatisfaction that I noticed Peter Sinclair, a Brasenose economics professor, every time we passed each other in one of the college quads. He always had such a kind smile for me, as he did for all of the students. Anybody who met him could feel that he was this incredibly benevolent soul. One day at the end of my second year, I woke up with the realization that there was absolutely no way I could study law for another day. It felt as if an inexorable force had welled up in me until this wasn't even a debate.

These moments of clarity are so rare in life, and even the people closest to us may question whether we should act on such instincts. I believe it's crucial to pay attention to these nonrational convictions that percolate inside us even if we can't explain them. My academic training—with its emphasis on hyperrational analysis—would deny the value of these almost inexplicable instincts and yearnings. But we need to respect these deeper recesses of our minds. This is not dissimilar to the way George Soros learned to tune in to his acute back pain as a signal that "there was something wrong" in his portfolio. Who is to say where the mind ends and the body begins?

I felt a similar sense of clarity and certainty when I decided to marry my wife, Lory. I knew with all my body and soul that we should be together. I had the same absolute clarity when I discovered value investing: I didn't *think* this was the right path for me; I simply *knew* it. I'm convinced that Warren Buffett makes his investment decisions the same way, performing an extraordinarily complex set of analyses almost unconsciously.

Every one of us has a handful of moments like this in the course of a lifetime. But we need the courage to act on them.

In any case, I walked into Peter Sinclair's office and asked if I could study economics as part of the PPE (Politics, Philosophy, and Economics) curriculum. To this day, I have no idea what possessed him to say yes and help me make the change. But I feel endless gratitude toward him because that single act may have done more to transform my life than anything else. The minute I became a PPE student, I started to feel connected to the world. Instead of reading up on turgid case law, my workload now felt like an in-depth exploration of what lay behind the day's headlines. It was a powerful example of what happens when we heed Joseph Campbell's injunction to "follow our bliss": new paths open up, and we feel a joy at being alive.

But before long, I was floundering again. Even though I enjoyed the subject tremendously, I faced a major disadvantage: two years into my university career, I hadn't studied politics, philosophy, or economics for a single day, and I had no idea what I was doing. Within months, the academic authorities informed me that if I didn't improve my performance, I might be expelled for academic reasons. The chilling Oxford term was to be "sent down."

Feeling hopelessly ignorant, I would stay up for most of the night trying to cobble together a half-decent essay. I knew how far behind the other students I was. One of them was the future British prime minister, David Cameron, who was highly intelligent and articulate, and superbly prepared by his years at Eton. We'd sit together in an economics tutorial with three or four other students, and I felt intimidated to speak in front of him because he was so much better informed than I was about British history and politics. Even the professors were impressed with him, whereas I had little clue about anything.

Students would sometimes banter about Cameron's erudite performances in his politics tutorials with Vernon Bogdanor, a renowned constitutional scholar who is now an advisor to both the queen and the prime minister. Apparently, Cameron and Bogdanor would launch into debates over which of the Victorian prime ministers, Disraeli or Gladstone, was a more effective leader. Hearing these tales, I felt woefully inadequate since I had scant knowledge of British history and barely understood the basics of the political system.

My way of competing was to focus ferociously on topics where I could stand out. I fell in love with political philosophy and spent countless hours debating and pontificating about John Rawls's theory of justice and other esoteric subjects. Fueled by fear of being sent down and exposed as stupid and undeserving of my place at Oxford, I learned to dazzle intellectually as a way of concealing my insecurities. I had a burning desire to be accepted and respected within this group of exceptionally smart people. This was fun when I was doing well and winning but not so much fun otherwise.

I was driven in large part by what Warren Buffett calls "the outer scorecard"—that need for public approval and recognition, which can so easily lead us in the wrong direction. This is a dangerous weakness for an investor, since the crowd is governed by irrational fear and greed rather than by calm analysis. I would argue that this kind of privileged academic environment is largely designed to measure people by an external scorecard: winning other people's approval was what really counted.

So during those formative years I was developing a serious flaw that I would later need to identify and reverse. Value investors *have* to be able to go their own way. The entire pursuit of value investing requires you to see where the crowd is wrong so that you can profit from their misperceptions. This requires a shift toward measuring yourself by an "inner scorecard."

To become a good investor, I would need to come to an acceptance of myself as an outsider. The real goal, perhaps, is not acceptance by others, but acceptance of oneself.

Of course, I didn't realize this back then. So I focused on mastering the rules of that exclusive academic world. I learned to think on my feet and come back with quick, sharply worded answers that would require my peers and professors to pay attention to me. To some extent, I still operate this way: when I get stressed or feel insecure, I revert to the dazzle-them-intellectually mode that I learned at Oxford. Only later would I see that this hard-earned skill was only really useful within the narrow confines of a university and a few other intellectually elitist environments. Someone like Mohnish doesn't have all of these dazzling skills. But he's way smarter than I am and educated himself in ways that are far more practical and effective in the real world.

And here's the rub: what was the point of having studied and appreciated the deep elegance of Rawls's theory of justice if I was so obtuse that I couldn't see that D. H. Blair was a snake pit? Even once I finally realized that I'd dug myself into this hole, it took me several unnecessary months before I galvanized myself to climb out. How is it possible that I could be so well educated and yet not have the common sense or moral courage to get out of D. H. Blair instantly?

Our top universities mold all these brilliant minds. But these people—including me—still make foolish and often immoral choices. This also goes for my countless peers who, despite their elite training, failed to walk away from nefarious situations in other investment banks, brokerages, credit-rating agencies, bond insurance companies, and mortgage lenders. For university educators, a little soul-searching would also not be remiss.

My study of economics at Oxford did at least develop my technical skills and my ability to reason. I eventually learned to analyze and tease out the implications of various economic policies. Some of this technical knowledge is not only intellectually elegant, but is also of inestimable practical importance to anyone who wants to understand what policies drive economic success. But there are also economic theories that, for all of their elegance, turn out not to be useful at all in the real world. I didn't have the ability to evaluate them critically, and this academic environment wouldn't have rewarded such heresy. So I swallowed everything wholesale, without question.

The most important example of this is the efficient-markets hypothesis, which is a powerful and theoretically useful assumption about how the world works. This hypothesis holds that financial prices reflect all of the information available to participants in the market. That has profound implications for investors. If it were true, there would be no bargains in the stock market since any price anomalies would be instantly arbitraged away.

In the real world, this is simply not true. But it took me a decade to realize it. Some aspects of my economics curriculum were so valuable that I somehow assumed that it was all equally valid. Part of the problem was that I had sharpened my ability to appeal to the academicians who graded my papers instead of training my mind to solve real-world problems. My professors neglected to ask seriously whether the efficient-markets hypothesis reflected reality—so I could safely neglect this question too.

I clung to this wrong-headed assumption with such unquestioning certainty that when I first encountered Warren Buffett at Harvard Business School a few years later, I had no interest in him at all. After all, if the market were efficient, the whole endeavor of searching for undervalued stocks would be futile. In my pursuit of academic success, I had narrowed my mind to such a degree that I was incapable of perceiving what was in front of me.

In this again, I'm a symptom of a broader problem. The very institutions that we have established to teach us to think independently often close our minds in potentially damaging ways. Charlie Munger discussed this very problem in a classic talk he gave at Harvard Law School in 1995 on the "Twenty-Four Standard Causes of Human Misjudgment." He described how B. F. Skinner influenced an entire generation of psychologists to espouse behaviorism in spite of plenty of disconfirming evidence. As the joke goes, "Science advances one funeral at a time" as eminent but wrong-headed scientists bite the dust.

At Oxford, it didn't matter that I was misguided in equally fundamental ways. Despite my real-world ignorance, I graduated first in my class in economics. If you stop and think about it, that should be a cause of some concern. Nonetheless, my self-confidence—and my arrogance—soared.

With my shiny new credentials, I scored a plum job at a strategy consulting firm called Braxton Associates. The senior management had all attended Harvard Business School, so I applied a couple of years later and was accepted.

At HBS, the curriculum is devoted exclusively to studying real business case studies. Rather than focus on theories of how the world *should* work, we focused on practical discussions of what had actually happened. This approach to educating leaders is far more robust and practical than the Oxford model as each case study provides a new set of facts and circumstances to analyze, creating a useful reservoir of experience. But Harvard also accentuated my hubris. To use an Indian phrase that I love, I was a "topper," and my glossy academic credentials reinforced my feeling that the world owed me a living in return for my general awesomeness.

In my first semester at Harvard, Warren Buffett came to speak at the business school. In my ignorance and arrogance, I instantly dismissed him as some speculator who had just gotten lucky. After all, the theoretical models I'd learned at Oxford made it a self-evident truth that searching for undervalued stocks was pointless, given that markets were efficient. For me to grasp that he'd made a fortune precisely by exploiting market inefficiencies would have required me to ditch all of my painfully acquired academic models. And so I did what many people do when the facts disagree with their theories: I dismissed the facts and clung to the theory. What I might well have said to him at the time was, "Mr. Buffett, don't confuse me with the facts, because I already have my firm opinions about efficient markets."

But if the truth be told, I was only in the lecture room at all because I was chasing after a woman in the second year who'd upset me by going out the previous night with another classmate. I didn't even sit down during Buffett's lecture, and I can't remember a single word he said.

It's a tragicomic reminder that my fragile ego mattered far more to me than the opportunity to learn. By contrast, part of what makes Warren himself so successful is that he's never stopped seeking to improve himself and that he continues to be a learning machine. As

Munger has said, "Warren is better in his 70s and 80s, in many ways, than he was when he was younger. If you keep learning all the time, you have a wonderful advantage." Back then, however, Buffett was utterly wasted on me.

Still, as the saying goes, when the student is ready, the teacher will appear. Sure enough, Warren Buffett reappeared in my life four years later when I stumbled upon his introduction to *The Intelligent Investor* and then read about him in Lowenstein's biography.

By then, I was going through hell at D. H. Blair. My arrogance had taken such a beating that I was open to Warren's teachings in a way that I never would have been as an MBA student. I had been so humbled and humiliated by my experience at D. H. Blair that it forced me to reexamine everything I believed. Such are the sweet uses of adversity.

There is, of course, a certain irony here. Joining D. H. Blair was the worst decision of my life. But it was also a gift—not only because this humiliation opened my mind but also because my experience there taught me lessons I could never have learned in the classrooms and quadrangles of the finest universities. In fact, D. H. Blair may paradoxically have been the perfect place for me to start my career because it showed me, in a raw and unvarnished form, everything that was wrong with Wall Street. I saw up close the willingness to distort the truth in order to further one's own narrow self-interest—the tendency to treat clients as marks to be exploited, not served.

At their worst, elite investment banks like Goldman Sachs and J. P. Morgan are not all that different. But the shafting of clients happens with a much greater veneer of respectability.

When I began to understand the principles that Warren Buffett embodied, I realized that there was another way to succeed. This discovery changed my life.

3

THE FIRE WALK

My First Steps as a Value Investor

AFTER LEAVING D. H. BLAIR, I HAD THE HARDEST TIME finding another job. There was this stain—a damned spot on my hitherto pristine résumé that I couldn't wash out. I had mistakenly given D. H. Blair the benefit of the doubt, but prospective employers were, understandably, not willing to give me that same benefit.

My résumé was strong enough that I could land interviews with companies like Goldman Sachs, Sanford Bernstein, and Credit Suisse First Boston. But I was damaged goods, and none of them would hire me. Wall Street insiders who understood D. H. Blair's reputation looked at me like this: either I'd been too stupid to figure out what was going on, or I was a dangerous fellow who was willing to push the boundaries of what was prudent. Either way, they wouldn't touch me.

I felt a growing sense of despondency as the rejections piled up. In the deepest emotional recesses of my brain, words like "rejection" and "can't find a job" were closely connected to words like "failure" and "leprosy." I really *did* start to feel like a leper. Then there was my inner critic. The voice inside my head that said, "What's the point in doing this? It's not going to get you anywhere." Or the more toxic version of this negative self-talk: "There you go again, you moron, you're always failing. You'll never have a successful career in finance."

But before long, I would find a way to get unstuck and begin re-wiring myself. The details of how this happened are specific to me, but the process relates to anybody who has been stuck and needs desperately to find a way forward. In a sense, what I really needed to do was reeducate myself. Or, for that matter, un-educate myself.

This process began in the most unexpected way, with my discovery of the self-help guru Tony Robbins. His name had come up in a conversation with a very smart Swiss couple who had PhDs from Stanford. I prided myself on being a serious thinker with a powerful grasp of economics and finance. My intellectual snobbery made it easy to dismiss someone like Robbins. With all my education, how could I possibly learn anything valuable from this crass American?

I don't think I would have been willing to find out more about Robbins if these friends had not been Europeans with stellar academic pedigrees. I hate to admit this because it exposes the shallow intellectual values that I had at the time. For me, the beginning of wisdom was to drop these narrow prejudices so that I could begin to learn from everyone.

I had been planning to spend the weekend hanging out and relaxing in San Francisco. But one of my Swiss friends, Diana Wais, told me that Robbins was doing a seminar there and that it would change my life. The title of the event was "Unleash the Power Within." I was full of misplaced skepticism, but I was able to get out of my own way sufficiently that I showed up.

In retrospect, I've come to see that this is a smart strategy for life: whenever I have the choice of doing something with an uncertain but potentially high upside, I try to do it. The payoffs may be infrequent, but sometimes they're huge. And the more often I pick up these lottery tickets, the more likely I am to hit the jackpot. This is an application of a powerful philosophy that Mohnish describes in his book *The*

Dhandho Investor: The Low-Risk Value Method to *High Returns*. As he puts it, "Heads, I win. Tails, I don't lose much."

Looking around the convention center on the outskirts of San Francisco, I wondered what the hell I was doing there. This looked like some kind of cult, with about two thousand people in the audience. What sort of self-promoting quack was this guy Robbins—and what sort of motley loser crowd had he gathered around him?

Robbins himself struck me as a rugged, quintessential Californian. He was almost seven feet tall and his energetic delivery was infectious. Many people in the audience were jumping up and down, yelling out things like: "Yes! Yes! Yes! I am a force for good!" And: "Step up! Step up! Step up!"

This set off alarm bells in my head. Was Robbins just some poor player, strutting and fretting his hour upon the stage? Was he just an idiot telling his story, full of sound and fury, but signifying nothing? I stood at the back, barely participating. But over several hours, in spite of myself, I found that I was opening up to the possibility that he had something to teach me.

Robbins won me over in part by being transparent about his motives. At one point, he told us, "Look, I'm an American just like you. My motivation is to be happy and successful and to live the best life I can. And like most of you, I also want to make money and be rich. Richer than I am today. A big part of how I do that is by running seminars like this. But as much as I want to get richer, even more than that, I like helping people. And I know that I can teach you things that will help you, and that are worth much more than the entry fee."

It was a great example of the power of authenticity—of speaking honestly and from the heart. His candid admission of his own self-interest convinced me to give him the benefit of the doubt. So I stayed.

In some ways, my original misgivings were right. Robbins seminars *are* a form of brainwashing. Shouting things out often enough really does pound it in, and any idea can be implanted by repeating it over and over. There's a danger to this—one that can be exploited by religious fundamentalists and political extremists. But in this case, it was brainwashing for the good, designed to help us live a better, more successful life. I'm all for that sort of brainwashing.

Our consciousness changes our reality, and I began to see that the positive statements Robbins got us to repeat were a powerful tool in reconfiguring my consciousness. Since then, I've often found that we have to imagine our future before it happens.

The power of human consciousness was illustrated in an unforgettable way that first night of the seminar. Robbins had whipped us into a mood of intense joy combined with extreme determination. In this altered state we stepped onto a lawn outside the convention center, removed our shoes and socks, and literally walked on red-hot embers. I don't know what the rational or scientific explanation is for why our feet didn't burn. But for many of us, this was a transformative experience. I could see the difference in people's eyes afterwards, as if a new fire and passion had been ignited in them—and in me.

Hokey as it might seem, this 20-foot fire walk created a metaphor for how I could break through my limitations and build a better reality. It was an experiential lesson that allowed me to understand how, as Robbins puts it, "Life can change in a heartbeat." A goal that seems impossible in one instant can become entirely possible in the next if only you are willing to devote every ounce of your mind, body, and soul to reach it.

My empirically minded Oxford professors—who had done so much to train me in the ways of logical thought—would have been amused and bemused at the impact on me of this motivational speaker. But his message was exactly what I needed to hear at a time when my formal education had led me to a professional dead end.

For example, Robbins hammered into my head the idea that, if you want to get somewhere, anywhere, and you're stuck, "Just Do It! Just make a move. Any move!" This might be obvious to many. Hell, it was obvious to me. But my bias toward analysis-paralysis meant that it was easier for me to pontificate in a library than to act. Robbins convinced me that I had to break the patterns of negative thought, push through my fears, and get moving.

As Theodore Roosevelt told an audience in Paris in 1910, "It is not the critic who counts; not the man who points out how the strong man stumbles, or where the doer of deeds could have done them better. The credit belongs to the man who is actually in the arena, whose face is marred by dust and sweat and blood."

Having opened up to Robbins, I started voraciously reading books by other self-help gurus. Before attending his seminar, I would have rolled my eyes at a book entitled *How to Win Friends and Influence People*. But Warren Buffett himself credits the author, Dale Carnegie, with having helped him enormously. In fact, Buffett has said that the only diploma he keeps in his office is a certificate confirming that he had "successfully completed the Dale Carnegie Course in Effective Speaking, Leadership Training, and the Art of Winning Friends and Influencing People." I would have been equally dismissive of *Think and Grow Rich* by Napoleon Hill, even though it had won over Prem Watsa, the highly successful chairman and CEO of Fairfax Financial Holdings, who is frequently described as "the Canadian Warren Buffett."

For a while, these books became my life instruction manuals. I wasn't reading them to sound intelligent at dinner parties; I was mining them for useful ideas to implement in my life. They provided me with critical first steps in my education as a value investor and businessman, exposing me to a more practical way of thinking about human nature and how the world really works.

For example, Carnegie explains that the best way of convincing someone of something is to appeal to their self-interest. Likewise, he talks about the power of using people's names when you address them, and the importance of showing genuine interest in the person. These simple insights helped me to shift the way I interacted with people. Previously, I would have focused on deploying my intellect to show them how smart I was or to appeal to the rational mind. I was too clever by half.

I started using the lessons of the self-help genre in a conscious way, seeking to brainwash myself into new habits of success. I even changed the way I talked to myself and others. Instead of saying, "I feel sick," I'd say, "I'm looking forward to feeling better." Trite as it may sound, having a positive attitude is crucial because our minds have a way of moving toward what we focus on. Schools and universities are so dedicated to developing the intellect that we can easily end up ignoring these simple strategies that make for a happier and more productive life.

At around the same time that I was learning these ideas, I was also taking practical steps to get out of my rut. I joined the New York Society of Securities Analysts and started attending their lunchtime sessions in the World Trade Center. I'd rush across Zuccotti Park to get there, no longer having the time to dawdle with the chess players.

I also bought some software from the American Association of Individual Investors to screen for Ben Graham–style "net-net" stocks. I put together mock portfolios in Excel spreadsheets and updated the prices by hand each week. I felt a rush of excitement as I saw that many of the portfolios I had assembled did much better than the market as a whole.

I also invested in a subscription to Value Line and pored over the new issues. It was in these pages that I noticed a company called the Burlington Coat Factory, which seemed cheap and had a long-term financial record that impressed me. It was the first stock I ever bought. I was captivated by Graham's insight that a stock isn't just a scrap of paper to trade but a part ownership in a business. So I visited the company's stores in New York and Omaha with relish and excitement, feeling like a true capitalist whose money was at work in a real business. I knew almost nothing at the time, but I held on to the stock for a couple of years and made a small profit.

Meanwhile, I started to see that there was a small ecosystem of value investors out there who operated with the same sort of intellectual and moral integrity that characterized Buffett. They were the antithesis of some of the people I'd encountered at D. H. Blair: they eschewed hype, focusing instead on serving the long-term interests of their shareholders. I felt a burning desire to be a part of their world. One company in particular stood out in my mind as a bastion of this type of investing: Tweedy, Browne, which had been founded in 1920.

I dreamed of getting a job at a place like this. So I bought some shares in two of the company's mutual funds, then asked if I could come by to see the firm's offices in Manhattan. I had hoped they would hire me, but they weren't looking for an analyst—at least not one like me. Still, I felt the thrill of walking on this hallowed ground. I knew that Buffett's old friend Walter Schloss had worked out of an office here for decades and had racked up extraordinary returns.

Once again, I felt the sting of rejection. But they were kind enough to give me a copy of Buffett's classic essay "The Superinvestors of Graham-and-Doddsville." I brought it home and discovered in it the spectacular investment record of another leading value firm, Ruane Cunniff, which manages the Sequoia Fund. This was one of only two companies that Warren recommended to his clients after he closed his investment business in 1969 and returned his shareholders' money. Since its inception in 1970, the Sequoia Fund has risen by 38,819 percent versus 8,916 percent for the S&P 500 index.

Hoping to find a job there, I wrote a letter to Ruane Cunniff and was invited to their offices by Carley Cunniff, a director who was also the daughter of one of the company's partners. I was in awe of her. She had grown up in a world where Graham, Buffett, and intelligent investing would have been regular topics of conversation over the family dinner table, and she had become an exceptional analyst.

Carley, who passed away in 2005, was generous and gracious. Even though there was clearly no opening for me to work there and nothing I could do to help her, she took me around and introduced me to her colleagues. In doing so, she showed genuine care for me, and I was really touched. She also taught me a valuable life lesson: it's so important to show kindness and be helpful to people early in their careers, even when they have done nothing to deserve it. She saw another human soul, gave me the benefit of the doubt, and did what she could to help a fellow value investor.

One way to stay in this orbit was to buy shares in the Sequoia Fund. That would enable me to attend its annual meetings each spring at the New York Athletic Club. But the fund had been closed to new investors for many years. So I found someone on eBay who was willing to sell me a single share for $500 even though the net asset value was only $128. I then added to my position. I expect to keep these shares for the rest of my life.

For me, the goal isn't to make money, though I'm guessing Sequoia will continue to outperform. It's really a question of choosing to have certain people in your life (however tangentially) who embody the values you admire. As we will discuss in detail later, creating the right environment or network helps to tilt the playing field subtly in the right direction so that you become far more likely to succeed. Advantages are often created imperceptible step by imperceptible step, so it makes a difference to enter the universe of a firm like Ruane Cunniff.

Many of the Sequoia attendees were also Berkshire Hathaway shareholders, and sometimes even the Berkshire managers attended. As a result, I met Lou Simpson, whom Buffett had handpicked to invest GEICO's money in stocks and whom he once described as "the best I know."

Another cornerstone of my reeducation involved studying Buffett's investment strategy with even greater intensity. There's no better way to do this than to read Berkshire Hathaway's annual reports. In those pre-Internet days, that meant calling up the company and giving them my address over the phone. A few days later, my first copy of a Berkshire report, addressed by hand, arrived. It was a revelation.

At D. H. Blair, I'd reviewed so many business plans with hockey-stick charts and predictions that only went up. Berkshire's report came with a plain cover, and its highlight was a candid, non-promotional, easily understandable letter by Buffett. The report also featured a table showing the annual increases in the company's book value. It was pure information, not an attempt to lie with statistics or to sugarcoat the truth with pretty pictures printed on glossy paper.

I'd never seen a report like this. It was designed to attract shareholders who were genuinely reading it for the right reasons. I'd assumed that the business world was all about shouting louder than the next guy so you could get attention. But Buffett was reaching out to people who weren't impressed by noise.

As I read and reread a compilation of Berkshire's old annual reports, I began increasingly to think as Warren Buffett would. I know this sounds odd, but I felt that he was smiling on me whenever I behaved in a way that he might have behaved; and I felt as if he had turned away from me whenever I strayed from that path. This wasn't a matter of idol worship. It was about choosing a teacher who had already discovered the truths that I still needed to learn.

There is a wisdom here that goes far beyond the narrow world of investing. What I'm about to tell you may be the single most important secret I've discovered in all my decades of studying and stumbling. If you truly apply this lesson, I'm certain that you will have a much better life, even if you ignore everything else I write.

What I stumbled upon was this. Desperate to figure out how to lead a life that was more like his, I began constantly to ask myself one simple question: "What would Warren Buffett do if he were in my shoes?"

I didn't ask this question idly while sitting in a coffee shop sipping a cappuccino. No. I sat down at my desk and actively imagined that I was Buffett. I imagined what the first thing would be that he would do if he were in my shoes, sitting at my desk.

Robbins describes this process as "modeling" our heroes. The key is to be as precise as possible, picturing them in as much detail as we can. A related technique that he teaches is called "matching and mirroring," which might involve changing the way you move or even breathe to match the other person's movement or breathing. In my experience, you start to feel what they feel and you even start to think like them.

This might sound peculiar, but the ability to mimic is one of the most powerful ways in which humans advance. Just think about how children learn from their parents. Given that this is a natural human instinct, it's important to be careful about whom we choose to model. The truth is, they don't even need to be alive. As Charlie Munger has explained, it also works "if you go through life making friends with the eminent dead who had the right ideas."

Luckily for me, this isn't a scientific book, so I don't have to prove or explain any underlying science (if there is any). But I can tell you authoritatively that, on a subjective level, this has worked for me. The minute I started mirroring Buffett, my life changed. It was as if I had tuned in to a different frequency. My behavior shifted, and I was no longer stuck.

So how can you apply these insights? We all know that mentoring is a big deal. Students and young professionals are often told to seek out mentors, just as those of us who are further along are supposed to find people to mentor. That's all well and good if your heroes are accessible. Mine wasn't. Buffett wasn't sitting in his office in Omaha waiting for a call from this tainted graduate of D. H. Blair. Thankfully, this didn't matter. I could get many—if not all—of the benefits of having him as a mentor by studying him relentlessly, and then imagining what he would have done in my shoes.

Imagining that I was Buffett, I also began to study the companies in his portfolio, wanting to see them through his eyes and to understand why he owned them. So I ordered up the annual reports for his major holdings, including Coca-Cola, Capital Cities/ABC, American Express, and Gillette. This again gave me that uncanny feeling that Warren—and perhaps God Himself—was smiling at me.

Then the annual reports started to arrive. I vividly remember reading the report for Capital Cities/ABC. Until then, I had never looked closely at the accounts of such a successful media company. When I saw the cash-flow statement, I found it hard to believe my eyes. The company was swimming in cash, and the income statement didn't come close to conveying the might of this cash-generating machine. Most of the companies I'd analyzed as an investment banker were either hemorrhaging cash or grossly overstating their cash-generating ability. It felt as if I were embarking on a second MBA.

I then decided to attend Berkshire Hathaway's annual meeting. Through a friend of a friend who was already a shareholder, I got hold of a ticket and flew out to Omaha, not knowing a soul who would be there.

I felt a rush of excitement on seeing Kiewit Plaza, the building where Buffett works—where the magic happens! I rented a car and drove past his pleasant but nondescript house with that same giddy sense of childlike joy. I also dined at his favorite restaurant, Gorat's Steak House, sitting with a group of Berkshire shareholders who were also in Omaha for the first time. In investing terms, I had emerged from the desert, crossed the Red Sea, and found my promised land.

There were two particularly memorable meetings for me in Omaha that year. One of them was with Rose Blumkin, a Russian Jewish immigrant who had founded the Nebraska Furniture Mart in 1937, using $500 that she'd borrowed from her brother. She transformed it into America's largest home furnishings company, and Berkshire bought a 90 percent stake in 1983 for $55 million, based on a handshake, without even auditing her books. Buffett later declared, "Put her up against the top graduates of the top business schools or chief executives of the Fortune 500 and, assuming an even start with the same resources, she'd run rings around them."

When I met Mrs. B, as she was known, she was 101 years old. But she was still an unstoppable force. She was a tiny lady driving a cart, surrounded by admiring fans who clearly bored her. When I got the chance, I looked her in the eye and asked, impertinently, "So, Warren tells me you sell carpets. Can you make me a good price?" Her eyes lit up. "Aha," she replied. "Are you a real customer, or do you just vont to make small talk like all zese ozer peeple?"

In that instant, I could see why Warren revered her. She was all business, all the time, and she was completely transparent. She had briefly tried to retire at 95, but had soon gone back to work. Her motto was: "Sell cheap, tell the truth, and don't cheat nobody." Just as I wanted Warren Buffett in my life, this is the sort of person he wanted in *his* life. Over decades, he had created this environment. I was just beginning to create mine, and I was learning to discern the type of people I should have in it.

The other encounter was with the oracle himself, shortly before the annual meeting began. I was on my way into the toilets and who was coming out but Warren? He smiled at me and said, "I always get a little nervous before these things." And then he walked on.

When I had last seen Buffett in person, back when I was a student at Harvard, I couldn't be bothered to listen to him at all. Now I was excited to see him coming out of the men's room!

Given his success, I had half-expected him to be a distant figure. It hadn't occurred to me that he'd be so personable and down to earth to a total stranger. Even from this brief encounter, I could see the goodwill he harbored toward his shareholders. Throughout the meeting, I could also see that he had no pretenses, no airs and graces. He is who he is.

Inspired by Robbins and Buffett, I had a growing sense of opportunity. Instead of feeling that every door was closed, I started to realize that it was possible to move forward. I was so obsessed with value investing that I hoped somebody would hire me as a stock analyst. But I still couldn't get a job.

Then, out of nowhere, my father called from his home in London to suggest that I manage some money for him. It was 1996. At the time, he was probably the only person who would have trusted me, given my D. H. Blair blemish. Born in Israel to German refugee parents, my father, Simon Spier, had founded a small but successful company, Aquamarine Chemicals, which trades and distributes products to protect crops. He had seen my mounting fascination with investing, and he told me, "Guy, if you don't break out on your own now, you'd be completely nuts."

That push got me started. He entrusted me with about $1 million. Within a year or so, he invested more, and two of his business associates invested alongside him. As a result, the fund's initial assets amounted to around $15 million. I named it the Aquamarine Fund, feeling that I was somehow rejoining the family business. The fund started trading on September 15, 1997.

For the longest time I wanted to hide or, at least, obfuscate this aspect of my journey. I desperately wanted to prove to the world that my achievements were entirely my own, and it seemed like an unfair advantage to get started with my father's help. But I was grateful for this opportunity—and daunted by the responsibility. In a couple of years, I went from being a Buffett wannabe to managing the overwhelming bulk of my father's life savings, along with assets from a small circle of friends and relatives.

Even with this backing, my odds of success were small. The vast majority of hedge funds don't survive beyond 18 months, and it's tough to make it without enough assets to achieve scale. To cut costs, I ran the fund out of my apartment in New York.

It was a pretty modest beginning. But I felt that I was finally doing what I had been born to do. Still, now the real test would begin: would I succeed in turning all this theory into the elusive goal of long-term, market-beating returns?

4

THE NEW YORK VORTEX

SO I STARTED RUNNING MONEY FOR FRIENDS AND family. I was 30 years old and relatively inexperienced. But there were a few things that I got right. In part, this involved figuring out what to avoid.

Warren Buffett, quoting Henry Ford, often talks about the importance of keeping all your eggs in one basket, then watching that basket very carefully. One thing that appalled me and that I'd seen too many times was the Wall Street practice of having many eggs in many baskets. Even the most reputable mutual fund companies have a practice of selling multiple funds. The ones that do well are those that then get the marketing dollars and raise more money from investors. The ones that do poorly are either shut down or merged into the better-performing funds. In the process, the failures are buried as if they'd never existed while the successes are highlighted.

I'd seen a similar thing happen at D. H. Blair. There, the brokers would put different clients into different stocks. The clients whose accounts went down would be a lost cause, but those whose accounts went up were good for more business. Similarly, the publishers of some investment newsletters have a practice of segmenting their mailing lists and sending different predictions under different titles to different people. They can then make hay with those segments of their overall mailing lists that have done well.

These ruses disgusted me then and they do now. I was determined that I would go through my entire investing career running only one fund so that I would have just one track record. Period. If the long-term performance of that fund is lousy, this will be obvious to everyone; there's no place for me to hide.

Equally important, my family's money would also be in that one fund alongside my investors' money. Indeed, I've invested almost 100 percent of my net worth in the Aquamarine Fund. As a result, I'm truly eating my own cooking. This alignment of my own interests and my shareholders' interests is inestimably important. This isn't a sales pitch. It's simply a matter of pointing out that this approach is conducive to good investing, not least because it enables me to focus on that one portfolio instead of having scattered interests. In this, I consciously modeled Buffett, who has focused all of his investing energy on Berkshire Hathaway for decades.

But there were other ways in which I deviated from the hard-won principles that he had taught me. For example, I should simply have copied the fee structure of his pre–Berkshire investment partnerships. He charged no annual management fee, but took a quarter of the profits above a 6 percent hurdle. This is an extremely unusual structure, but it's the best alignment I've ever seen between an investor and his shareholders. It truly embodies the principle of making money *with* them, not *off* them. Unless they do well, the fund manager earns nothing.

However, in starting the Aquamarine Fund, I opted instead for the standard New York hedge fund fee structure. This meant that I'd receive a 1 percent annual management fee (which would reward me however poorly I performed for shareholders), plus an incentive fee of 20 percent of the profits.

Why did I do this? In getting the fund going, I was inevitably surrounded by lawyers, brokers, and other advisers who all wanted to tell me how this game works. To them, the idea that I would adopt Buffett's unorthodox 1950s fee structure seemed outlandish. They wanted to protect me, explaining that I needed that steady income; they couldn't conceive of someone living off incentive fees that are entirely unpredictable. What they didn't see was that the 1-and-20 fee structure subtly misaligned my interests and my shareholders' interests. I allowed myself to be swayed by them, but I should have been more pigheaded in this case.

I also wanted to copy Buffett by allowing investors to redeem their money only once a year. This helps the fund manager to invest for the long term, which benefits his shareholders. It also helps them psychologically because they think less often about how the fund is doing and whether to sell. After all, inaction and patience are almost always the wisest options for investors in the stock market. For the same reason, I find it better not to check the performance of my stocks every day (or, for that matter, every week) since this makes it harder to keep a long-term focus.

In any case, my advisers thought this redemption policy was absurd. They insisted that I allow investors to redeem with just 30 days' notice. The trouble is, this means that the fund manager is always worrying about when shareholders can yank out their money. Later, when the market crashed in 2008, this structural flaw would prove to be a major vulnerability.

Failing to stand my ground, I capitulated and accepted that these were well-established practices in New York hedge fund circles. The whole institutional environment made it hard for me to resist. In spite of my good intentions, I fell into a common trap: it's always easier to be with the crowd than to go against it. It gave me false comfort to know that this was the "industry standard" even though I'd missed the opportunity to create the ideal structure.

It was only later—when I met Mohnish Pabrai, and again when the financial crisis hit—that I saw how much better it would have been to clone Buffett's partnership structure as precisely as possible. These misguided compromises weren't deadly sins. But when I look back on my investing career, it's painful to see how quickly I had allowed myself to drift away from the time-tested wisdom I had gained from Omaha.

I could have gotten it totally right. A perfect score. I still had a solid passing grade, but these tiny differences matter in investing—a pursuit where small structural changes can add up to big differences in returns over time. Long-term compounding is an investor's best friend, so why get in its way? There's a huge benefit to getting these seemingly minor details right from the very start.

Part of the problem was that it was so easy to get sucked into the vortex of the New York financial world, with its skewed values and seductions. I felt that my mind was in Omaha, and I believed that I could use the force of my intellect to rise above my environment. But I was wrong: as I gradually discovered, our environment is much stronger than our intellect. Remarkably few investors—either amateur or professional—truly understand this critical point. Great investors like Warren Buffett (who left New York and returned to Omaha) and Sir John Templeton (who settled in the Bahamas) clearly grasped this idea, which took me much longer to learn.

At the time, I thought about moving to Omaha myself, but I had too many connections in New York that made me want to stay. Still, in those first years after getting started, I mostly kept aloof from the New York scene and from Wall Street. I worked in blissful isolation out of my one-bedroom apartment on West 66th Street and then in a series of three informal office spaces.

One of these was an apartment on West 58th Street, where Monica Lewinsky was a neighbor. Another was a two-bedroom apartment on West 55th, where David Neeleman, the founder of JetBlue, was my neighbor. I'd read that he, like me, had attention deficit disorder (ADD). Yet he'd still managed to build a successful company. I found this reassuring: having him in the building was a frequent reminder that I could also overcome my idiosyncratic wiring. As investors, we all have shortcomings; as I came to see it, the key is to accept who we are, understand our differences and limitations, and figure out ways to work around them.

In the meantime, even without a professional-looking office, life was good. The fund was still tiny, but my investment returns were decent. The performance was driven by the success of stocks like Duff & Phelps Credit Rating, which rose seven-fold. It illustrated perfectly what I had learned from Buffett: find companies that are cheap, that have an expanding "moat" around them, and that are awash in cash.

While others got caught up in the tech bubble of the late 1990s, I didn't get lured in at all, partly because I was in the orbit of cool-headed investors like Buffett, Ruane Cunniff, and Tweedy, Browne. Their common sense helped to protect me from tech fever. This proved once again that environment trumps intellect.

After five years, my fund had significantly outperformed the market. A slow but steady trickle of outside investors entrusted their savings to me. Eventually, Aquamarine's assets under management edged over $50 million, and I started to get noticed. I wasn't interested in Wall Street, but Wall Street was interested in me. And this was, at best, a mixed blessing.

I was now on the radar of all sorts of people who wanted a piece of me. Some hoped I would hire them as a lawyer or an analyst. Some wanted to sell me a high-priced investment research service. Some wanted to be my broker. Some wanted me to pay them to market the fund in order to attract more assets.

These people hoped that I might be the next Chris Hohn or Bill Ackman, who were rapidly gaining recognition as two of the brightest investment stars of my generation. And these people were betting that there was money to be made if I lived up to their expectations (or wishful thinking). After all, I'd attended Harvard Business School with Chris and Bill, so there was a sense that I might be cut from the same cloth.

I was dangerously flattered. Worse, all this attention had the effect of stimulating some macho desires in me—competitive juices and testosterone that I hadn't felt in myself since my early days as an investment banker. After all, if all these marketing mavens, ambitious analysts, lawyers, and brokers were comparing me to Bill and Chris, why shouldn't I make the same comparison? I still remember one of them telling me that I should be running $5 billion, not $50 million. At some level, it was as if my very manhood was in question.

At the time, Bill and Chris were going from strength to strength. Based on their stellar returns, they *were* running billions, while I was still a minnow. Before long, I felt a deep, avaricious need for size and status. The green-eyed monster had gotten the better of me, and I was consumed with envy.

This is an oversimplification of many crosscurrents, but it captures a key component of my New York vortex. Until that point, I hadn't ever experienced envy in such a visceral way, and I didn't recognize it at the time. But that's what it was.

Buffett and Munger joke that envy is the only one of the seven deadly sins that isn't any fun. "Envy is crazy," remarks Munger. "It's 100 percent destructive. . . . If you get those things out of your life early, life works a lot better."

In my view, envy is also an emotion that we deny at our peril. In the financial markets, envy is a silent killer: it leads people to behave in ways they wouldn't if they were more honest with themselves. For example, investors see their friends make a killing off tech stocks that are crazily overvalued, and they plunge in right before the bubble bursts. It's important to be aware of these emotional forces bubbling inside us since they fundamentally skew our judgment, messing with our ability to make rational decisions. As an ancient rabbinical saying puts it: "Who is strong? He who masters his own passions."

Ben Graham wrote brilliantly about the irrationality of Mr. Market. We need to recognize that this irrationality is also an inextricable part of our all-too-human wiring. A key aspect of my education as a value investor was to learn to detect these emotional vulnerabilities in myself so I could develop strategies—as we will see later—that prevent them from subverting me. This process of self-correction begins with self-knowledge.

The reason all of this matters is that investing has a way of exposing our psychological fault lines—whether it's greed, a lust for power and social status, or any other flaw. Envy was one of my biggest weaknesses at the time. I should have been happy with my lot, given that I wasn't just a member of the "one percent" but the one percent of the one percent. I was in control of my time. I could live and vacation where and when I wanted. I had people to help me do the things that I didn't like to do.

But the problem in a place like New York or London is that there are always so many people who are doing better than you. My office didn't have gleaming floor-to-ceiling windows or panoramic views of the Manhattan skyline. I couldn't match the elegance of Chris Hohn's offices in Mayfair, London's hedge fund epicenter. My beautiful home on one of the Upper West Side's loveliest streets lacked Bill Ackman's leafy views of Central Park.

I wanted to win at the hedge fund game. Rightly or wrongly, I was convinced that I was as smart as my peers, and it ate away at me that I wasn't at the very top of the heap. Doing well didn't feel like enough.

I decided to market myself, but I didn't know how. On those rare occasions when I did get an audience with potential investors, I'd get nervous and revert to the behavior that had worked for me at university, blasting out a torrent of ideas at high speed in the hope that I'd sound impressive. Sometimes I'd find myself trying to dazzle people with Latin phrases like "ceteris paribus" and "sine qua non," hoping they would see the merit of what I was saying if I spoke as if I were in a tutorial at Oxford.

But the truth is that I shouldn't have bothered with this mindless pursuit of growth, which was primarily motivated by my own ego. The fund was doing well, and so much of my family's money was invested in it that I didn't need to waste time attracting additional assets from outside investors. My envy led me astray because I wanted people to see that I was managing hundreds of millions, even billions, just like Bill and Chris. That time would have been better spent focusing on picking the best stocks and allowing my performance to speak for itself.

I got sucked into the New York vortex in other equally ridiculous ways. I rented a plush office in Carnegie Hall Tower, and in one fell swoop drove up my annual rental expense from $60,000 to $250,000. I rented a Bloomberg terminal—the informational equivalent of smoking crack cocaine—for about $20,000 a year. I also hired a chief operating officer, an analyst, and a high-powered lawyer. It turns out that envy and pride are expensive flaws.

But it wasn't just a matter of winning other people's approval. It also made me feel better about myself to have the trappings of success. I needed to know that I was on top, so I kept chasing after these false idols. My father wisely asked me, "Why are you doing all this? Why are you trying to be a hedge fund megastar?"

Fortunately, I got plenty of other stuff right. Among other things, I didn't play roulette with my shareholders' money, having internalized Buffett's teaching that the first rule of investing is "Don't lose money," and the second rule is "Don't forget rule number one." I was relatively risk-averse in a way that served the fund well, particularly during the tech crash. But I think it's more helpful to share my mistakes with you than to dwell excessively on what I got right. As Munger puts it: "I like people admitting they were complete stupid horses' asses. I know I'll perform better if I rub my nose in my mistakes. This is a wonderful trick to learn."

There are plenty of things I regret about that period in New York. But I made one decision that would prove hugely beneficial: I began to surround myself with a "mastermind" group of investors who would become life-long friends and trusted sounding boards. It's difficult, if not impossible, to become successful on your own. The greatest opera stars have singing teachers; Roger Federer has a coach; and Buffett meets regularly with like-minded people.

Our forum, which we dubbed "the Posse," met once a week to discuss stocks. It included investors like David Eigen, Ken Shubin Stein, Stefan Rosen, Glenn Tongue, and occasionally Bill Ackman. Through it, I also met Joel Greenblatt and became a member of the Value Investors Club. The Posse met one morning a week, and at least one of us had to come prepared with a stock idea, which the rest of us would debate and dissect. This expanded my knowledge beyond anything I could have learned from a textbook or MBA course. We not only learned more about investing but gained a deeper understanding of each other—about what made us tick, or not tick.

The Posse's meetings produced friendships that are a reward in their own right. From a pure investing perspective, these allies have also become a source of competitive strength because we look out for each other. If I call members of that group and run an idea by them, it's not just what they say that's important; my knowledge of them also allows me to evaluate the information they give me. It's critical that we understand one another's biases and filters.

On one memorable occasion, this group saved me from myself—and reinforced for me the benefit of being open to other perspectives.

I had discovered what I thought was a fantastic company. It was called Farmer Mac. One way that I look for investments is to study the masters and then explore whether I should buy the same stock or a better one with similar characteristics. Buffett had a huge investment in Freddie Mac and a substantial stake in Fannie Mae. Both companies would subsequently lose their way. But at the time, Freddie and Fannie were great businesses. Their key asset was the implied faith, backing, and credit of the US government, which meant they could borrow at virtually risk-free rates. I looked for a firm with a similar advantage and found Farmer Mac—a tiny government-sponsored enterprise in the US farm sector. It struck me as an undiscovered gem of the same ilk.

In 2003, I invited the company's management to give a presentation to the Posse. Whitney Tilson, who is a well-known hedge fund manager, author, and TV commentator, later shared the idea with Bill Ackman. Bill, who started an investment firm called Gotham Partners after graduating from Harvard, is a brilliant analyst with an extraordinary gift for seeing what other investors miss.

A few weeks later, Bill took me aside after a breakfast meeting with the Posse and said. "Guy, there's something I want to talk to you about." Knowing his generosity and his relish for acting as a matchmaker with his single friends, I was convinced that he wanted to set me up on a date. In fact, he wanted to tell me more about Farmer Mac, having heard that I owned the stock. Apparently, Bill had stayed up until about 4:00 a.m. researching the company after Whitney mentioned my interest in it. The next morning he phoned Whitney and thanked him for "the most incredible opportunity I've ever seen." But it turned out that Bill wasn't buying the stock: he was shorting it. In other words, he was convinced that Farmer Mac was going to implode.

As we walked about 20 blocks to his midtown office, Bill explained what he thought I was missing, and why he'd established a massive short position. He thought the stock was not just going to implode, but fall to zero. He proceeded to tell me why Farmer Mac was nothing like Freddie and Fannie. I felt my stomach turn. Seeing that I didn't yet fully understand, he invited me up to his office. There, to my amazement, he showed me a shelf filled with more than a decade's worth of printed filings for Farmer Mac. These were covered with annotations and sticky notes. He had also printed out the filings for many of the company's securitizations.

At first glance, they seemed just like Freddie and Fannie's securitizations. But, as Bill explained, they were actually very different. In Freddie and Fannie's case, one securitization typically contained hundreds, if not thousands, of similar single-family homes. In Farmer Mac's case, the securitizations often contained only a handful of farm loans, each with very different characteristics. Bill's view was that this was not an asset that could be securitized and that this was really more like regular business lending. As he saw it, these packages of loans were far riskier than they seemed, and the company could easily go bankrupt.

At one point, I said to him, "But this is a government-sponsored enterprise. It's almost like an arm of the US government." Bill replied, "Guy, you have far too much trust in the institutions of our country."

As lunchtime approached, I found myself torn between a desire to stay with him and learn more and a compulsion to rush back to my office to sell the stock. By now it was absolutely clear to me that I didn't understand nearly enough about Farmer Mac to justify owning it. This was an important revelation: so often, we focus our analytical efforts in the wrong direction and miss something vital. So it's crucial to be open to the possibility that we might be mistaken. During our charity lunch, Buffett looked at me in all seriousness and said of his investment analysis, "I'm never wrong." In his case, this might be true, or almost true. But as the hedge fund manager Lisa Rapuano once said, "I'm not Warren Buffett and neither are you."

That day, I sold two-thirds of my holding; the next day, I dumped the rest. Luckily, I was able to sell out at a profit.

I subsequently arranged a meeting with Farmer Mac's CEO and CFO. On a rainy autumn afternoon, I met Bill and Whitney at Penn Station, and we took the Acela train to the company's headquarters in Washington, DC. The management team was ready with a standard investor presentation, which emphasized the superficial similarities between Farmer Mac, Freddie, and Fannie. After one or two slides, Bill put up his hand and said, "Please, we don't need to go through your presentation. I just have a few questions."

He then made the same points he had previously made to me. The management was either unable or unwilling to respond to Bill's probing questions, and they were clearly offended. At one point, the CEO said, "This might not be the company for you." I was shocked to see that he couldn't come up with a more compelling response.

A week later, I shorted the stock. This was one of only three occasions in my life when I've gone short. Temperamentally, this practice doesn't suit my nature. But, to my mind, the management's reaction confirmed that Bill was right. Afterward, he told me that they had even excluded him from the company's quarterly conference calls.

I started to get carried away with the whole combat sport of shorting a stock. I got on these conference calls myself and asked pointed questions designed to highlight the company's weaknesses. I was determined to show other investors the risks that lurked behind the veneer. I also spoke to the *New York Times,* explaining these concerns. These were valid and important points, and investors had a right to know that the company was riskier than they thought. But there was a righteous (or self-righteous) indignation in my attitude that didn't reflect well on me.

In retrospect, I feel as if I lost my way and acted like a petty tyrant. My goal as an investor is to compound money for my shareholders, not to pick unnecessary fights or conduct myself like an avenging moral crusader. I'm not criticizing other fund managers who want to do this, but it's not my role in life, and I think it distracted my mind and muddied my hands.

Not long afterward, I got my comeuppance. The *Wall Street Journal* published an article suggesting that various hedge fund managers might be banding together to manipulate the price of stocks they were shorting. These included MBIA, Allied Capital, and Farmer Mac. Eliot Spitzer, who was then New York State's attorney general, launched an investigation, as did the US Securities and Exchange Commission. They wanted to know if any of the fund managers mentioned in the article had been involved in spreading misinformation about these companies.

I got roped into the investigation, along with Bill and the renowned hedge fund manager David Einhorn. The investigation went nowhere, but it was a stressful and expensive distraction, since I had to dig up lots of information in response to the investigators' research requests. During the financial crisis, all three stocks imploded, vindicating Bill's analysis. Farmer Mac proved to be a highly profitable short for him and me.

Still, I wish I had just sold the stock and walked away, regardless of the profits that came from betting against it. As I see it, life is too short for this sort of conflict, and these investment gains didn't justify the headache. Odd as it might sound, I also think we often bring bad things on ourselves when we point the finger at others or act in a tyrannical way. In my experience, it's karmically better to focus on the positive and act as a force for good instead of getting gratuitously embroiled in acrimonious battles. I wonder if Eliot Spitzer—who was himself later disgraced—discovered this same truth after years of crusading to take other people down.

I yearned to find a path that was simpler and better for my mental health. In New York, I had drifted off course, allowing myself to get caught up in a series of unnecessary distractions. But I was starting to realize that I didn't need a fancy office; I didn't need to attract more assets to my fund as a way of proving to others (and myself) that I was a big shot; and I didn't need the angst and acrimony that came with shorting stocks.

In other words, I had learned enough by now to sense what *didn't* work for me. But I still needed to find a better way. Little did I know that I was about to meet two masters of investing who would help to point me in the right direction.

5

MEETING A MASTER

IN MY EARLY YEARS AS AN INVESTOR, I WANTED TO BE a superstar and for other people to recognize my brilliance. By nature, I was a lousy salesman, but I came to understand that this was something I needed to learn. I started to explore how to market and sell myself more effectively. The result was strange and unexpected. What I learned about marketing would change me as a human being—so much so that I stopped caring about selling myself at all.

I had studied marketing at Harvard. But my true education in this field began when I attended the annual meetings of the Sequoia Fund. I became friends there with a delightful American businessman named John Lichter, who was an investor in both Berkshire Hathaway and Sequoia. He gave me a CD of Charlie Munger's talk at Harvard on the 24 standard causes of human misjudgment.

I quickly realized that I'd been handed a mother lode of wisdom that was unavailable anywhere else, and I resolved to listen to this lecture as many times as possible. It soon displaced my Tony Robbins recordings, and there was an 18-month period during which this was the only CD in my car's entertainment system. Munger has an astonishing mind. Mohnish Pabrai, who has spent time with him, later told me that Charlie is the smartest guy he's ever met—even smarter than

Buffett. What's more, Munger has an extraordinary grasp of different disciplines, and this speech distilled and integrated his knowledge of psychology, economics, and business in a way that blew my mind.

For example, he spoke about the way that "extra-vivid evidence" distorts our thinking. During a crazy run-up in tech stocks, say, an investor sees that Yahoo! is skyrocketing and hears on CNBC how everybody is getting rich off these hot Internet investments. The investor's reptilian brain reacts irrationally to this extra-vivid evidence, making it harder to understand that the stock price no longer reflects the company's intrinsic value. This primitive wiring—which is deeply embedded in all of us—was helpful for cavemen faced with a wild beast or a fire, but it's woefully ill-suited to analyzing the nuances of the stock market.

Munger also explained that there's a "lollapalooza effect" when several forms of misjudgment occur simultaneously. For instance, when an investor sees friends and relatives making a fortune off Internet stocks, it provides a "social proof" that these investments are a great bet, since 10,000 lemmings surely can't be wrong. The investor's amiable broker then calls to tout these stocks; the fact that he's so likeable and that we have a built-in "reciprocation" tendency makes it even harder for the investor to resist his pitch.

It's difficult for professional investors, not just for amateurs who are new to the market, to resist this kind of lollapalooza of mind-bending distortions. We like to think we're immune, but these forces are so powerful that they constantly subvert our judgment. And these are just a couple of examples of the kind of misjudgments that trip us up. In reality, there are many more, often occurring simultaneously.

Munger helped me to understand these tricks that the mind plays on us, and I began to see these patterns all around me. Equally important, his speech mentioned Robert Cialdini, a renowned academic who had written a book entitled *Influence: The Psychology of Persuasion.* Munger said Cialdini's book had "filled in a lot of holes" in his own "crude system" of psychology.

Each year, on the first weekend in May, I'd make my pilgrimage to Omaha for Berkshire's annual meeting. I would typically stay at the Omaha Marriott, close to the heart of the action. The night before the meeting, Munger would host a private dinner there. I'd hang out in the lobby and watch with fascination as his eclectic group of guests passed by—people like Bill Gates, Ajit Jain, and Robert Cialdini. This reinforced my sense of Cialdini's importance, so I read and reread his books multiple times, consciously pounding in his message over and over.

What affected me most was an extraordinary story Cialdini told about a Chevrolet salesman, Joe Girard, who regularly wrote holiday cards to thousands of his former customers with the words "I like you" printed on each card, along with his name. This personal expression of goodwill had an unbelievable effect: Girard won a place in the *Guinness World Records* book by selling 13,001 cars in 15 years. As Cialdini writes, "We're phenomenal suckers for flattery," and "we tend to believe praise and those who provide it."

I was fascinated. Was it really that simple? Was it all just a matter of harnessing this "liking" principle? I have a tendency to go to the extreme: if an idea resonates for me, I don't just flirt with it—I embrace it to the nth degree. So I decided that I would write three letters per working day, or 15 per week. I began to thank people for giving a great speech, for sending me their investor letter, for providing a great meal in their restaurant, for inviting me to their conference. I would send people cards to wish them a happy birthday. I'd send them research reports or books or articles that I thought would interest them. I'd send them notes saying how much I'd enjoyed meeting them.

At around the same time that I read Cialdini's books, I also stumbled upon a book that included many of Ronald Reagan's letters. He wrote to an amazing range of people, and he seemed to have a genuine interest in every one of them. He shared jokes and advice, addressed their concerns, encouraged kids. It seemed to me that this was part of the secret of his success. He wasn't the most cerebral American president, but he mastered the art of caring for others, and he expressed his care through letters. If this had worked for the president as well as for America's top car salesman, I knew there was something in it for me.

At first, my letter-writing experiment was quite calculated, since I did it with an explicit desire to improve my business. I had a clear expectation of what the results would be. But it started to feel really good, and I became addicted to the positive emotions that this activity stirred in me. As I looked for more opportunities to thank people, I found that I truly did become more thankful. And the more I expressed goodwill, the more I began to feel it. There was something magical about this process of getting outside myself and focusing on other people.

Tony Robbins had taught me that small differences in how we behave can, over time, have a profound impact. And this small action of writing hundreds of letters a year was transformational for me. Initially, it wasn't easy. I often didn't know what to write or to whom. So I'd end up writing to my doorman or the person who'd served me coffee that morning. At times, I felt foolish. And I didn't see an immediate impact. My view now is that it can take as long as five years to have a significant effect, so most people give up long before they reap the benefits.

In sending out this cascade of letters, I began to open up to people in a way that I never had before, and I started to see everyone around me as someone I could learn from. As I now understand, this habit of writing letters is an incredibly effective way of compounding goodwill and relationships instead of merely compounding money. Einstein is often said to have called compounding the eighth wonder of the world. But the narrowly financial application of compounding may be the least valuable and least interesting aspect of this phenomenon.

My letter-writing crusade had begun as a way of marketing my fund, but it ended up giving me a richness of life that I could hardly have imagined. Rather than becoming a good salesperson, I found myself starting to care about the people I was writing to and to think about how I could help them. The paradox is that, as I became more authentic and discarded my agenda, people became more interested in investing in the fund. This was an unintended consequence of becoming less selfish and more honest about who I am.

A couple of years after I'd launched this writing campaign, I met a Wharton student named Aaron Byrd. He was a lovely guy, and I felt an immediate connection to him, so I invited him to do an internship with me. Later that summer, Aaron told me that he was going to Chicago for the annual meeting of an investor named Mohnish Pabrai. I'd never heard of Mohnish, but Aaron said he had phenomenal investment returns. So I decided to go along.

As I later learned, Mohnish has a colorful background. He's the grandson of a well-known itinerant magician and the son of a businessman who had at least as many failures as successes. Born in 1964, Mohnish grew up in Mumbai, New Delhi, and Dubai and arrived in the United States as a penniless student in the 1980s. He went on to build an IT consulting and services business called TransTech, which he financed with $70,000 in credit card debt and about $30,000 from his 401k. TransTech's revenues grew to $20 million and he ultimately sold the company for $6 million.

Like me, Mohnish discovered Warren Buffett and value investing through the Lowenstein biography and by studying Berkshire's annual "Letters to Shareholders." He was so captivated that, in 1999, he set up his own investment firm. The returns of the Pabrai funds have been superb. In September 2013, *Forbes* published an article headlined "How Mohnish Pabrai Crushed the Market by 1100% since 2000."

Back in 2003, when I attended his annual meeting in Chicago, it was already clear that he was something special. He had been compounding capital at more than 30 percent per year. But I was equally struck by his understated and idiosyncratic way of conducting business. Anyone in the New York investment world has been to their fair share of "rubber chicken lunches." These tend to be held in fancy hotels like

The Pierre, and they involve a manager or management team presenting all of the reasons why you should buy their stock or fund.

The Pabrai meeting was completely different. It wasn't held in an elegant downtown hotel but in a Carlucci restaurant with an auditorium, conveniently located near Chicago's O'Hare Airport. Also, it took place over the weekend. The guests were dressed casually, and some had even brought family members with them. This was typical of Mohnish. He didn't bother to conform to people's standard expectations. He wasn't fearful of being different, but his unconventional decisions made total sense to me.

During the meeting itself, he went over the fund's performance, then provided a couple of examples of his investment approach: one success and one failure. The audience, which included about 100 people, wasn't there to be pitched. They were there to learn. Mohnish spoke honestly and straightforwardly, unafraid of what anyone might think about him.

I was particularly struck by his discussion of a successful investment he had made in Frontline Ltd. I sat there taking notes at a furious rate while he explained that he had invested at a time when its oil-shipping tankers were trading for less than their replacement cost. I understood well the concept of buying assets at less than replacement value, but he gave me a deeper insight into the mechanism by which the low price itself would be a catalyst to turn the market around since the supply of tankers was drying up. In doing this, Mohnish exhibited what Howard Marks would later call "second-level thinking"—a grasp of nuance that is important but rare among investors. Mohnish had a different perspective on the world than others, but his rationale for making this kind of contrarian investment was utterly persuasive.

For a detached observer, it was an interesting scene. For example, I could see that two people in the audience were basically there to promote themselves. In one case, a fund manager positioned his question as a way to tout his own record. An investment banker was also clearly out to promote his own services. I could sense the unease with which most of the audience responded. A good meeting is always a team effort. But these two were there to sell, not to learn, and they came across as brash.

By contrast, Mohnish came from a place of personal abundance, which was not merely a matter of financial wealth: he was comfortable with who he was, and he was happy to share his wisdom. Characteristically, he has since moved from a house in a posh California suburb to a more modest home that's closer to his office. To me, this is evidence once again that he doesn't measure himself by what Buffett calls an "outer' scorecard," and this is a considerable source of strength.

After Mohnish's annual meeting, I returned home to New York, picked up a fountain pen, and wrote him a short note. Written in my semi-legible scrawl, it said something like: "Dear Mr. Pabrai, Thank you so much for having me as a guest at your partnership meeting. I learned a lot about life and investing, and I also met some great people. Warm regards, Guy Spier."

It was one simple note out of at least a dozen letters that I sent that week. I had no agenda in writing it and expected nothing in return. I mailed it and then forgot about it. But Mohnish later told me that I was the only person who wrote to him after that meeting, and my note clearly stuck in his head. About six months later, he sent me an email to say that he was going to a meeting in Greenwich, Connecticut. Did I want to meet for dinner? I most certainly did.

That meal with Mohnish altered the trajectory of my life—even more, perhaps, than my subsequent lunch with Warren Buffett. If I hadn't bothered to thank Mohnish, many great things that have happened since our first dinner might never have occurred. I didn't understand this at the time, but I now see that every letter I wrote was an invitation for serendipity to strike. To many people, it might seem like a waste of time. But I couldn't win the lottery without a ticket, and these tickets were almost free. In a sense, this is a value investing approach to life: pick up something cheap that may one day prove to be precious.

We met at the Delamar Greenwich Harbor Hotel. I arrived half an hour early with a sense of anticipation, flattered that this remarkable investor had reached out to me. At that stage in my life, I still tended to go into meetings with a self-interested idea of how I wanted it to turn out. But I consciously showed up that evening with no agenda. I resisted the temptation to dominate the conversation with a slew of my own questions designed to reverse engineer what he had done to generate such high returns. I was just grateful for the opportunity to hang out with him.

Perhaps Mohnish sensed this, and it helped to set the right tone. When you have an agenda, people smell it, and this tends to put them on the defensive. Strange as this may sound, I feel as if I had some kind of divine inspiration that enabled me to understand that I needed to be myself with him. His own authenticity made me see the foolishness of being fake or insincere.

What I saw during that meal was a man completely at ease with himself. The person on the outside was the same as the person on the inside; he wasn't pretending to be anything to anybody. So often in my life, I wasn't aligned or at peace with myself. But in Mohnish's presence, from the very start, I was myself. Misalignment is a dangerous thing, not just in relationships but in business and investing. For example, Charlie Munger points out that it's always easier to be truthful because you don't have to remember your lies. This relieves your brain of much unnecessary mental work so that it can focus on something more useful.

Mohnish talked to me during that meal about a book called *Power vs. Force: The Hidden Determinants of Human Behavior*. The author, David Hawkins, explores the theory that we have a greater capacity to influence others when we're an authentic version of ourselves since this truthfulness evokes a deep psychological response in others. Mohnish himself seemed to embody this idea that real power resides with a person who is honest and in touch with himself. Our discussion planted a seed in me: in the future, I wanted to be truly authentic, completing the transformation I had begun when I left D. H. Blair and that whole world of lies.

I quickly realized that Mohnish, like me, had been on a quest for worldly wisdom. But he had arrived at it from a different direction and with a very different mind. From Tony Robbins I had discovered the power of modeling the habits of successful people; Mohnish, who referred to this as "cloning," sometimes jokes that he's never had an original idea in his life, but this doesn't bother him in the least. Indeed, this is often the way progress works: we copy the best ideas and make them our own.

Mohnish understood that this applies to businesses too. Companies can profit richly by studying their competitors, figuring out what they do well, then recreating it. He used the example of two gas stations on either side of the same road. One has a smart owner who provides a full serve at a self-serve price, doing things like cleaning windscreens and checking fluid levels for free. In other words, the owner constantly takes small actions that improve the business, creating a virtuous cycle. The gas station across the road fails to do these things and languishes. Yet, as Mohnish pointed out, it would be easy for the owner of the bad gas station to copy everything that his more successful rival is doing. Many of the best ideas are already out there for us to see; we just have to clone them.

This is what Mohnish and I had also learned to do in our investing careers. We saw what Buffett had done, and we consciously sought to copy him. But Mohnish was a much better cloner than I was, thanks to his relentless attention to detail. For example, he had carefully replicated Buffett's original investment partnerships, including their fee structure and redemption terms; it took me more than a decade to understand that I should have done this myself when I opened my fund.

During our dinner, I joined Mohnish in pitying the fools who fail to copy the great ideas that are already out there. But a few years later, I was humbled to realize that I resembled the owner of the gas station on the other side of the road while Mohnish was the owner of the more successful gas station. As we will discuss later, I eventually wised up and learned from him.

My next meeting with Mohnish had an even greater impact on my life. I had no idea whether he'd enjoyed our dinner as much as I had, so I was delighted when he emailed me some months later and asked me to join him for breakfast in New York. He was there to give a presentation at the Value Investing Congress. I wanted to make sure that our meeting was memorable since I intuitively knew that it was important to my life. I picked the restaurant at the Mandarin Oriental Hotel, which has stunning views over Central Park and was convenient for Mohnish's conference. The day before our breakfast, I even visited the restaurant to make sure that we'd have a good table and that the bill would be presented to me, not to my guest.

This might sound over the top. But it's an illustration of something I had learned from Mohnish: some businesses succeed because they get one thing right, but most succeed because they get a lot of small things right. This is what made a company like Wal-Mart so successful. A key aspect of my real-world education involved learning to take more and more of these intelligent but practical actions on a micro level: writing thank-you notes, picking a great place for breakfast, listening actively to what people told me, or treating them the way I wished to be treated. Over a lifetime, a myriad of simple actions like these can accumulate to create big reputational and relationship advantages. It's not about luck. It's about working harder to get these things right so that it becomes more likely that something good will happen.

The breakfast was wonderful. At first, I was in awe of Mohnish. After all, my investment returns were good and I had a decent intellect, but his returns were spectacular, and his mind is so exceptional that it made me feel pedestrian. We also have different cognitive styles: I can be scatterbrained, with a mind that darts all over the place, while he's totally directed. But we had much in common, including a deep-seated sense that we were both outsiders. I came from a family of Jewish refugees from Germany who had achieved success in Israel and England; he was an Indian immigrant who had made it big in America. For whatever reason, I felt increasingly connected to him both emotionally and intellectually, even though I was sure that I had nothing to teach him.

As we sat by the window at the Mandarin overlooking the park and the Manhattan skyline, Mohnish raised an idea that had never occurred to me. He wondered if we should join forces to bid for a charity lunch with Warren Buffett that is auctioned on eBay each year. At first, I thought it was insane to spend hundreds of thousands of dollars on a single meal, even with an investor who had already changed my life. I tried to be polite, remarking, "That seems like an awful lot to pay for a lunch. Why would anybody do it?"

This was a conventionally sensible point, but Mohnish patiently walked me through his unconventional analysis of why it made all the sense in the world to bid for the lunch. He pointed out that the money would go to a very worthy charity, the GLIDE Foundation, with the added benefit of lunch with Warren thrown in. As Mohnish understood, so many charitable donations come with nothing more than a meaningless plaque featuring the donor's name, which is designed primarily to burnish their reputation or inflate their ego. In this case, the donation would bring with it something infinitely more valuable: a meeting with a towering role model who offers a far more enlightened example of how to be a capitalist.

Mohnish also helped me to see that there was no need to seek anything tangible from the lunch. Rather, it was our opportunity to enjoy Buffett's company and thank him for everything he had taught us. By the end of breakfast, I was totally convinced.

So we agreed to team up and bid together for the lunch with Buffett. That first year, we lost the auction to a higher bidder. But the following year, Mohnish was determined to bid again. I was traveling in Europe when he rang me on my mobile phone. "Guy," he said. "This time we've got to win it."

If we won, the plan was that Mohnish would bring his wife and daughters with him, while I'd be joined by my wife alone, as our children were too young to attend. Since there would be more Pabrais than Spiers at the lunch, Mohnish kindly proposed to pay for two-thirds of whatever it cost, while I would pay for one-third.

Even so, I was worried that the bidding might get out of hand. I was still a young money manager running a small fund, and Lory and I were expecting our third child, so we might need to move to a bigger home in Manhattan. I told Mohnish that I was good for $250,000 but said that I didn't think it was prudent for me to go beyond that. If the bidding went above $750,000, as he expected, I might well have to drop out. Mohnish paused for a moment. Then he assured me that, if this happened, he'd cover the balance himself so that my contribution would be capped at $250,000. I was flabbergasted by his generosity.

We didn't even shake hands on this deal, let alone draw up a written agreement. I found this level of trust deeply touching. It reminded me of the way that Buffett himself had often made financial agreements with barely a written document. Nobody in business other than my father had ever treated me this way.

In the end, we won the auction at our second attempt, with a bid of $650,100. I was so excited—and so anxious for Mohnish not to think that I might let him down—that I wired my third of the money to the GLIDE Foundation the very next morning. Only then, once the money had gone through and it was a fait accompli, did I call Mohnish to tell him how ecstatic I was.

Our lunch was set for June 25, 2008. This would give me several months to prepare myself—just enough time, I hoped, to make sure that I was worthy of meeting the grand master himself. After all, if you're going to meet someone better than you, you had better work on yourself first.

6

LUNCH WITH WARREN

FOR SEVERAL YEARS NOW, I'D BEEN MOVING CLOSER to Warren Buffett's orbit. In the late 1990s, as tech stocks soared, Berkshire Hathaway lagged, and there was plenty of misguided muttering about how he had "lost his touch." The skeptics wondered why he stuck to his supposedly outmoded style of investing in unsexy—but highly profitable—businesses while the herd made a killing off hot tech stocks that traded at crazy multiples of their revenues.

Amid this insanity, Berkshire's unfashionable stock slumped to what struck me as an irrationally low price. So I loaded up, investing over 20 percent of my fund in the company. Since then, the stock has more than quadrupled while many of those once-hot tech darlings have gone the way of the dodo. Berkshire has remained a big investment for me, providing an important anchor for my fund, and it's still capable of generating high returns for many years to come.

In the meantime, I was constantly striving to model Buffett's way of thinking and investing. I read about him incessantly, studied the stocks he bought, and did my best to replicate what made him great. By the time of our charity lunch, I had also visited Omaha about a dozen times to attend his annual meeting.

In those early years of going to Omaha, I was still stuck in my New York vortex, so I typically hung out at the Omaha Marriott with other high-finance types from the Big Apple. This gradually changed. Instead of mingling with the New York crowd, I began to stay at the DoubleTree Hotel, joining the members of a Buffett fan club called the Yellow BRKers. Their website warns: *"The Yellow BRKer Gathering is a 100% informal and unofficial gathering of Berkshire shareholders. The gathering is not intended as a forum to promote any particular product [or] service."*

The people in this group weren't dressed for success, and they didn't have the slightest interest in doing business at the Berkshire meeting. They were there to learn, to celebrate friendship, and to drink from the well of wisdom. These were primarily amateurs who had invested their own money in Berkshire. In many cases, they had owned the stock for decades. They had a different energy from that of my New York colleagues—professional investors and networkers who often wore a standard uniform of khaki pants and blue blazers.

Through Mohnish, I also met various Indian fans of Warren, some of whom had traveled thousands of miles to be in Omaha. I liked hanging out with all these nonprofessionals who weren't interested in dealmaking or working the room. They didn't take themselves too seriously, and we became a raucously funny gang. For me, the values and ethos of this understated group seemed healthier and more down-to-earth.

Instead of showing up in my jaded and superior Oxford-Harvard-New York mode, I allowed myself to let go and join the fun as just another Buffett fan and disciple. On the day of the annual meeting itself, I no longer strolled in at the 8:00 a.m. start time so that I could avoid the rush. Instead, I began to get up at 5:30 a.m. so that I could join the hard-core faithful in a line by the south door of the convention center.

As a result, I would find myself sitting with Mohnish at the front of the room, enjoying a perfect view of Warren and Charlie. This was a much better place from which to learn than the back row, where I had previously been a more passive and even judgmental observer. As I had come to realize, if you're going to do something, it's best to commit to it with wholehearted gusto. Other serious investors—including Prem Watsa, Li Lu, and Mario Gabelli—had clearly come to the same conclusion because I found them at the front too. Once again, the point is that these small actions make a major difference at the margin.

Other than my one decidedly brief exchange with Buffett as he left the men's room in the Omaha convention center, I had never had any personal interaction with him at all. For all these years, I'd simply watched him and studied him from afar. But my letter-writing campaign—which had led to my meeting with Mohnish and then to our successful bid for the charity lunch—now propelled me into a whole new realm of possibility. Suddenly, I was about to meet my hero in person, for lunch!

It seemed unreal. I was only just beginning to align myself with the universe, and I hadn't even done that much that was right. But when you begin to change yourself internally, the world around you responds. I hope this idea resonates because it's important—more important, perhaps, than the fact that I had lunch with Warren Buffett. As I hope you can see from my experience, when your consciousness or mental attitude shifts, remarkable things begin to happen. That shift is the ultimate business tool and life tool.

I had already changed a lot in the years since D. H. Blair. But there were aspects of my hedge fund's business model that were still misaligned. As the lunch with Buffett approached, I felt a growing sense of discomfort about this. A part of me feared that he would see me and recoil at the sight of just another greedy hedgie from New York, reaming investors by charging a 1 percent annual management fee and 20 percent of the profits.

Mohnish didn't charge an annual management fee; he got compensated only if his shareholders did well. As for Warren, his annual salary for running Berkshire was $100,000—almost comically low given the many billions of dollars in profits he had made for his fellow shareholders. So I'd be showing up at the lunch with the highest fees and the most self-serving fee structure despite running the least amount of money and having the lowest returns of the three of us. It's painful to write this, but it's true.

I could have tried to exculpate myself by pointing at the many hedge fund managers who charge a 2 percent annual management fee. But the fact that their fee structure was even more egregious than mine gave me little comfort. I wasn't the worst offender, but I wanted to be on the right side of the line. Buffett wasn't aware that he was having this impact on me, but he set such a great example with his own fee structure that he made me want to treat my own shareholders more fairly. This was part of the power of the mere expectation of meeting him.

There's a joke on Wall Street that a hedge fund is really just a fee structure in search of an investor to fleece. I didn't want to be part of this system, but I had allowed it to happen, buckling far too readily under pressure from advisers who had told me that this was standard operating procedure. Now, faced with the contrast between Buffett and me, I felt that it would be unbearable to show up at the lunch as the only person who charged an annual management fee.

So I instituted a new share class for my fund, mirroring the fee structure of Buffett's original partnerships. Existing shareholders could stick with the old arrangement if they preferred, but they now also had a better long-term option: in the new share class, they would pay no annual management fee, and I wasn't entitled to receive an incentive fee until after they had received a 6 percent annual return on their investment. Above that hurdle, I'd receive a quarter of the profits, getting handsomely compensated only if my shareholders did well too. I should have done this a decade earlier, setting myself on the right path from day one.

Smart investors innately understand why this new fee structure makes sense. So this shift would later have the benefit of attracting the right long-term partners for the fund without my trying to sell to people who couldn't grasp my real objective.

In my early days as a money manager, slick marketers wanted to help me sell the fund to more investors so that it would grow bigger and more profitable. This never really worked, and I was chasing after success in the wrong place. What ended up working best was to look inward, changing myself internally and putting my shareholders' interests before my own. As in so many areas, it took me years to learn what Buffett already knew.

Before our lunch, I also wanted to visit the GLIDE Foundation, the charity he had chosen to support. I was curious to see why he was donating his time to this particular organization. As I've come to understand, if you encounter someone who has exceptional qualities, it's worth investing the time and energy to travel so that you can be in their force field. GLIDE was in Buffett's force field, and I wanted to know why.

So I flew to San Francisco to find out more about this remarkable charity, which has the mission of creating "a radically inclusive, just and loving community." Among its initiatives, GLIDE runs a church in the impoverished Tenderloin district, provides health services, and serves over 800,000 meals a year to the needy. Warren had been introduced to GLIDE by his late wife, Susan, who was an extraordinarily generous soul. He began to support the charity by auctioning his annual lunch online, and he continued to do so after Susan passed away in 2004.

I was greeted outside GLIDE's headquarters by its beaming founder, Reverend Cecil Williams, a minister and social activist on behalf of the poor and marginalized. Here was a man who, like Buffett, did his job with every ounce of his being. Later I had lunch with him in GLIDE's soup kitchen, seeing for myself how he bantered with everyone and how they were drawn to him. It didn't take long to realize that this is a wonderful organization that extends genuine warmth and humanity to people who have given up on themselves. As Buffett once put it, GLIDE recognizes that everyone has "a potential, no matter what their circumstances. This is a proven process, that a combination of love and time and energy and resources can produce a different human being."

What also dawned on me was that Reverend Williams was a quintessential Buffett manager—not that different from the CEOs who run Berkshire's businesses. He was authentic to the core. There was no façade. He gave his own attention and energy to the people he helped. And he obviously relished his work. Later that day, I recorded a video for GLIDE in which I mentioned that Buffett was not just "a very discerning picker of businesses" but had also clearly identified "a very special charity."

More important, perhaps, the GLIDE visit showed me how concerned Buffett was with using his power to do good. His example encouraged me to keep looking outside myself to see who I could help—and the more I did this, the happier my life became.

According to the rules of the auction, Mohnish and I had specifically won a "power lunch" for seven people—plus Warren—at the Smith & Wollensky steakhouse in Manhattan. Our party would include Mohnish, his wife Harina, their two daughters Monsoon and Momachi, along with Lory and me. In other words, there were only six of us, which meant that there was technically a spare seat. Various acquaintances had approached me to buy that last seat. One London-based fund manager offered me $100,000 to join us. A swaggering private equity guy suggested that we give the seat to David Cameron and also disinvite our families.

When Lory heard about these bids, she selflessly offered to give up her own seat so that we could give it to someone who would value it more highly. But this wasn't a business deal, and her seat wasn't for sale. Still, I felt obliged to mention the $100,000 offer to Mohnish. He was adamant: this was a family event and a way of thanking Warren. There was no hidden agenda. Auctioning off the seats or allowing nonfamily members to come with us would have quickly destroyed that spirit.

At last, the day of the lunch arrived. It was a beautifully sunny morning in late June. Lory and I rode in a cab from our apartment to the restaurant, which is on 49th Street and Third Avenue. We arrived an hour early as I wanted to savor the moment and didn't want to be late for such an important occasion. Television cameras from CNBC and elsewhere were already stationed outside the restaurant. With Warren's permission, we had also hired our wedding photographer to memorialize the event.

I was so nervous that I was run down and had a cold. I knew that Buffett was a penetrating judge of character, and I was afraid of being exposed. What if he saw through me and detected any lingering remnants of the Gordon Gekko side of my nature? But I was also enormously excited. From my meals with Mohnish, I'd seen what a huge impact it can have simply to hang out with a person you revere. So I was thrilled at the prospect of seeing Warren up close, of observing what made him tick. This would be the ultimate capitalist master class.

At around 12:30 p.m., the seven of us sat down for lunch in a cozy, wood-paneled alcove near the kitchen. It was only semiprivate, and there was a buzz among the other diners when they peered into the alcove and saw that Warren Buffett was there. He wore a business suit, a white shirt, and a bright yellow tie with a black pattern. Mohnish's daughters sat on either side of him. I sat two seats to his right, between Momachi and Lory. Mohnish and Harina sat to Buffett's left.

It was lovely to have our wives and Mohnish's kids there since this made it a lighthearted and joyful family affair instead of a more formal business meeting. Warren, who had brought gifts for the two girls, beamed with pleasure and goodwill—more like an amiable grandfather than one of the world's richest men and the greatest investor of all time.

As I'd seen at Berkshire's annual meetings, he had no pretenses or stuffiness about him. Warm and friendly, he insisted on our calling him Warren and went out of his way to put us all at our ease. He asked the girls how old they were, and then replied: "You're 12, you're 11, and I'm 77." Then, when the menus arrived, he joked with the kids that he doesn't eat anything he wouldn't touch when he was less than five years old. Sure enough, he ordered a medium-rare steak, hash browns, and a Cherry Coke—an appropriate choice, given that Berkshire is the biggest shareholder in Coca-Cola. Not wanting to dwell on the menu, I followed his lead, ordering a steak, hash browns, and a Diet Coke.

Before the lunch, Buffett had obviously gone to the trouble of reading up on us. He asked Lory about Salisbury, North Carolina, where she was born, mentioning that he'd spent time there with a friend from his student days at Columbia University. He also made a point of saying how impressed he'd been by a remarkable annual report for Mohnish's charitable foundation, Dakshana, which educates children in India. He floored Mohnish by saying that he'd sent the report to Charlie Munger and Bill Gates. Indeed, when Buffett spoke to Fox News about our lunch, he specifically mentioned Mohnish's charity, remarking, "He thinks as well about philanthropy as he does about investments. . . . This guy has thought a lot about what he's going to do with the money he makes over time. He's going to turn it to the benefit of really, I think, thousands of people. . . . I admire him enormously."

It was clear that Buffett himself had thought a lot about what to do with his money. He talked to us about his thinking in setting up charitable foundations for each of his three children, and he added that "it's usually not a good idea to wait" to give money back to society: it's best to go ahead and do it now, he said, instead of compounding the money and giving a larger sum later. I joked that he was technically the least wealthy person at the table, since he'd already pledged most of his Berkshire Hathaway shares to the Bill and Melinda Gates Foundation; as a result, he was now working virtually for free, much like GLIDE's founder, Cecil Williams. He grinned happily and said that was "absolutely right." He seemed glad that I understood how little he cares about personal enrichment and how much he cares about using his wealth to help others.

When we thanked Warren for making this lunch possible, he said that he was excited to do it. For one thing, it gave him a great opportunity to honor Reverend Williams and also his own late wife, Susan. He said that he had known right away, at 18, that she was the person he wanted to marry, and that he would never have gotten where he is today without her. He spoke with tender admiration about her kindness, recalling how she had taken terminally ill AIDS patients into her home and given them her own bedroom, seeking to ease their pain in their final days. He told Mohnish's children that choosing the right person to marry would be the most important decision of their lives.

For three hours, we relished the most wonderfully wide-ranging conversation. For example, Harina and Mohnish asked Warren about Sir Isaac Newton, since he had once remarked that Newton was the historical figure with whom he'd most like to have lunch. He explained to us that Newton was "probably the smartest human in history" but joked that he'd thought this through some more and would actually prefer to have lunch with Sophia Loren. He said Charlie Munger would most like to share a meal with Ben Franklin, since "Newton was smarter, but Franklin was wiser."

At one point, Warren also spoke about a trip he'd taken to China with Bill Gates. Cruising up the Yangtze River, they had talked about a man whose job was to "drag the boats in" when they reached the dock. Warren recalled telling Gates that, no matter how smart that guy was, he'd never get a chance to do anything more with his life. He said that, in his own life, it would have been a major disadvantage to be born anywhere but the United States since he might not have read Ben Graham's *The Intelligent Investor,* which wasn't available then in any language but English. He said Graham's book *Security Analysis* had been his "holy grail," and added that he'd been amazed when he then discovered that Graham was teaching at Columbia. Hoping to grab Graham's attention, he wrote him a letter that said, "I thought you were dead."

Early in the conversation, I made a confession: I told Warren how I had changed my fee structure so that he wouldn't think I was just another greedy, two-and-twenty hedge fund guy. I also mentioned how hard it had been to convince my fund's lawyers that this un-orthodox approach made sense since it was fairer to my shareholders. I'll never forget Warren's response: "People will always stop you doing the right thing if it's unconventional." I asked if it gets any easier over time to do what's right. He paused, looked away for a moment, and replied, "A little."

He then went on to explain how crucial it is to adhere to values that you know to your core are right rather than being swayed by ex-ternal forces such as peer pressure. "It's very important always to live your life by an inner scorecard, not an outer scorecard," he said. To il-lustrate this, he then asked us, "Would you prefer to be considered the best lover in the world and know privately that you're the worst—or would you prefer to know privately that you're the best lover in the world, but be considered the worst?"

At that moment, I remember thinking, "Yes, that's true." But it was only later that I felt the full force of this advice. In the months that followed, I began to realize just how much of my life I had spent measuring myself by an outer scorecard. I had always been so eager for people to like and respect me—to win the plaudits of my professors at Oxford and Harvard, to be seen as a successful investment banker and deal maker at D. H. Blair, to be admired as a top-notch fund manager. This neediness had inevitably led me astray. What I really needed was to measure myself by an inner scorecard. For a start, this would have enabled me to run for my life the moment I realized how toxic it was at D. H. Blair.

It's hard to overstate the importance of Buffett's insight. After all, how many of the self-serving excesses and moral compromises that caused the financial crisis of 2008–2009 would have been avoided if mortgage brokers, bankers, and others had lived by an inner scorecard? As Warren helped me to understand, people too often justify their improper or misguided actions by reassuring themselves that everyone else is doing it too.

One of Buffett's defining characteristics is that he so clearly lives by his own inner scorecard. It isn't just that he does what's right, but that he does what's right for him. As I saw during our lunch, there's nothing fake or forced about him. He sees no reason to compromise his standards or violate his beliefs. Indeed, he has told Berkshire's shareholders that there are things he could do that would make the company bigger and more profitable, but he's not prepared to do them. For example, he resists laying people off or selling holdings that he could easily replace with more profitable businesses. Likewise, some investors have complained that Berkshire would be much more profitable if he'd moved its tax domicile to Bermuda as many other insurers have done. But Buffett doesn't want to base his company in Bermuda even though it would be legal and would have saved tens of billions in taxes.

This was one of the greatest lessons of our lunch. His strength comes in part from this rock-solid sense of who he really is and how he wants to live. There's no artifice. No need to live according to other people's standards or opinions. Sitting with him at Smith & Wollensky, I could see that he makes no compromises in terms of his own happiness—even in something as small and insignificant as his gleeful enjoyment of the restaurant's desserts. Clearly, he has set up his life so that it suits him and so that he enjoys it. When I asked if he had consciously created Berkshire's unique decentralized structure, he emphasized that it operates that way because it suits his personality, not because it maximizes returns.

As an investor, he has always remained true to himself. During the tech bubble, when so many other people got carried away, he had no trouble sticking to his principles, even though this meant that he massively underperformed the market before it imploded.

Likewise, it wasn't difficult for Buffett to resist the temptation to invest borrowed money, which could have made him richer but could also have landed him in trouble. Indeed, one of the key lessons of our lunch came when Mohnish asked what had become of

Rick Guerin, a friend of Buffett's whom he had mentioned in his article on "The Superinvestors of Graham-and-Doddsville." For a while, Guerin's investment record had been spectacular. But Warren told us that Guerin had been "in a hurry to get rich" and had used leverage to juice his returns. When the market crashed in 1973–74, Guerin was hit hard and was forced to sell various holdings, including thousands of shares of Berkshire Hathaway that would now be worth a fortune.

For Warren, the travails of this gifted investor clearly provided a powerful example of the perils of debt and the virtues of patience. "Charlie and I always knew we would become very wealthy," he told us, "but we weren't in a hurry." After all, he said, "If you're even a slightly above average investor who spends less than you earn, over a lifetime you cannot help but get very wealthy—if you're patient."

It helps that Buffett has created a peaceful environment for himself in which he can operate calmly and rationally. By staying in Omaha, he has remained far from the madding crowd. His legendary personal assistant Debbie Bosanek (who has worked at Berkshire for more than three decades) also helps to shield him from unnecessary distractions. She once told Mohnish and me that Warren usually keeps his cell phone switched off and doesn't even have an email address. The fact that he has the right filters clearly helps him to guard against letting in the wrong type of information.

Indeed, for all his charm and affability, Buffett doesn't hesitate to disengage himself from the world in order to avoid distractions that might impair his judgment. He told us that people often try to convince him to meet them so they can pitch investments to him, but he's comfortable saying "no" far more often than he says "yes"—regardless of their attempts to flatter him. He also told us that he typically avoids meeting corporate managements, preferring to rely on companies' financial statements.

Similarly, he chooses not to fill his days with distracting meetings. During our lunch, he showed us his appointment diary, which was mostly empty, and said he manages his schedule himself. By contrast, he said Bill Gates's calendar is filled with precise entries like "6:47 shower" and "6:57 shave." It's not that one system is better or worse: it's that Buffett has chosen a system that suits him perfectly, giving him the latitude to think in peace, impervious to the noise that tends to dominate Wall Street. As Buffett taught me, it's not enough to rely on one's intellect to filter out this noise: you need the right processes and environment to do so. For this reason, I decided to move to Zurich just six months after our lunch, knowing that it would be easier for me to remain clearheaded there, far from the New York vortex.

Thankfully, this is one aspect of what Buffett does that other investors can replicate: we can clone the environment and processes he has created to keep the noise at bay. For me, this has meant not only moving away from Wall Street, but blocking out other types of noise that would otherwise muddy my thinking. For example, I totally ignore market predictions and focus instead on investing in companies that should grow significantly over the long term. At lunch, I was happy to admit the extent to which I tried to study and clone Buffett's actions. I explained my attitude by telling him a Talmudic story about two students who were so eager to learn from their rabbi that they even slipped under his bed to watch him at night. Warren joked that he'd be checking under his bed from now on to see if I was hiding there.

But there is at least one aspect of Buffett that is entirely inimitable: his brainpower. During our lunch, I felt that his mind was operating on about five different levels simultaneously. His biographer Alice Schroeder has since described a similar feeling in his presence. It's hard to explain. But when I sat at the table with Buffett that day, I felt the sheer intensity of his mind and simply knew that he was operating at a much higher clock speed than I was. In the past, having come top of my class at Oxford, I'd somehow convinced myself that I had the mental capacity to compete with him, and I had hoped that I might one day learn to perform equally well. Seeing him in person that day, I was left with no doubt at all that I could never hope to match him.

This could have been dispiriting, but I found it weirdly liberating. For me, the lesson was clear. Instead of trying to compete with Buffett, I should focus on the real opportunity, which is to become the best version of Guy Spier that I can be. It reminded me of an old joke that Warren likes to tell: "How do you beat Bobby Fisher?" Answer: "Play him at anything other than chess."

I couldn't beat Warren at his own game. But I could certainly follow his example. What impressed me most about him that day was not just his mental firepower, but the fact that he lived in a way that was totally congruent with his own nature. Nothing seemed to be misaligned. He had evidently spent his life trying to be true to himself.

This became my own goal: not to be Warren Buffett, but to become a more authentic version of myself. As he had taught me, the path to true success is through authenticity.

7

THE FINANCIAL CRISIS

Into the Void

VALUE INVESTORS PRIDE THEMSELVES ON BEING ABLE to buy when the market is imploding. We like to think that we possess the calmness, courage, and strength—not to mention the intellectual clarity and understanding—to act rationally when almost everyone else is panicking. But what *really* happens when the market crashes and there's blood in the streets? I would find this out firsthand in 2008–2009 when the financial world tumbled into the void, dragging me and my fund with it. As Warren Buffett has said, if you weren't scared, you weren't paying attention. God knows I was scared.

The experience of the crash was sufficiently painful that it's difficult for me even now to write about it in a totally honest and forthright way. This isn't a conscious decision. There are memories from that time that I've no doubt suppressed because they are almost too wrenching to face. William Green, a friend and shareholder who is helping me to write this book, recently reminded me of a call we had back then in which I told him, only half joking, "We're bleeding from every orifice." I have no recollection of this at all. Still, there are certain moments from that time that are unforgettable even if I would prefer to forget them.

One of the worst of those moments came with the delivery of the *Financial Times* one morning in March 2008. Over breakfast, I read on the front page that Bear Stearns was teetering on the brink of insolvency. My fund was a brokerage client of Bear Stearns, and the firm held all of our assets in various accounts. I remember my wife, Lory, exploding at me because I was so distracted and had been totally ignoring my family. I turned to her and said: "Don't you get it? All of Aquamarine's money is in Bear Stearns. It could all disappear tomorrow."

I spent much of that weekend in my office, researching the names of experts who, come Monday, could advise me on what it would mean for the fund if Bear Stearns went bankrupt. I needed to know what would happen to our accounts, whether it was possible that they could be frozen for years while a bankruptcy trustee sifted through the rubble of the firm.

As a conservative, risk-averse investor, I had intentionally placed all of our securities in Bear Stearns cash accounts that were fully owned by our fund. I knew that borrowing money and investing on margin can be catastrophic since a brokerage firm can then take control of the assets in a margin account and sell them at the worst possible moment. This is effectively what had happened years earlier to Long-Term Capital Management.

I had been maniacally focused on avoiding such risks, acutely aware that I needed to protect our assets, and I didn't have a single cent of leverage or debt—either personally or in the fund. Bear Stearns was simply our custodian, which meant that our cash accounts were theoretically not vulnerable at all. Even so, the unpredictability of the situation was terrifying. In reality, who could say what would happen to these segregated accounts if Bear went under? All bets were off.

I was sitting at my desk in my office in Manhattan on the afternoon of Sunday, March 16, watching financial history unfold. The office was eerily quiet. Everything seemed to be happening in slow motion. I knew that I wasn't in control, that my fate was in the hands of Hank Paulson, Ben Bernanke, and other policymakers whose sole interest, rightly, was to protect the global financial system—not me, my fund, or my investors. Potentially, almost all of my family's net worth was at risk, along with the savings of dozens of friends, relatives, and business associates. Even so, in this moment of crisis I felt strangely calm.

All of a sudden, my Bloomberg monitor came to life, lighting up with a news flash that JPMorgan Chase had decided to acquire Bear Stearns. I reached for the phone and called my father to share the news. Later that evening, I dialed into a conference call and listened with overwhelming relief to Jamie Dimon's assurance that JPMorgan "stands behind Bear Stearns . . . guaranteeing [its] counter-party risk." Never have such prosaic words meant so much to me. Even as I write this, I feel a wave of emotion.

The Bear Stearns bullet, which I had not even known to exist until a few days earlier, had come appallingly close. But we had been saved. I've never met Jamie Dimon, but I've sent him a Christmas card every year since. I once saw him at a cocktail party in Davos and didn't speak to him, but I was tempted to go over to him and give him a hug.

Another ordeal that is seared into my memory occurred in September 2008. We had just returned from a wonderful family vacation in Europe. Lory and I had recently had our third child, and we were happily ensconced in a new apartment on Manhattan's Upper West Side. Then, on that sunny September afternoon, my father phoned me out of the blue to ask if I thought Lehman Brothers would go bankrupt. Most of his money was invested in the Aquamarine Fund. But it turned out that he had also stashed a sizeable chunk of his liquid assets in Lehman Brothers bonds. Now it looked like Lehman was in a death spiral.

I was almost speechless. We had recently escaped disaster with Bear Stearns—and now this? I paced around my living room, listening to my father in disbelief. "Lehman Brothers bonds? You bought Lehman bonds! Why?"

I couldn't imagine how he could possibly have stepped into this minefield. Less than a year earlier, I had listened to a superb presentation on Lehman by David Einhorn at the Value Investing Congress. He had picked apart the bank's financial statements to show just how vulnerable it was, so I knew not to touch it with a ten-foot pole. Yet I now discovered that my own father had invested a significant sum in Lehman bonds without thinking to tell me.

He explained that a financial adviser from one of the world's largest and most prominent banks had called him up to recommend these bonds, assuring him that they had a triple-A rating from Moody's. He had felt particularly confident in buying them because he was aware that Moody's was one of my holdings, and he knew that I invested in companies with good products.

But I understood exactly how this game worked. Professional investors were fleeing from Lehman in droves. So the Wall Street selling machine had kicked into high gear, touting this dross to overly trusting clients. With Lehman's usual investors shunning its bonds, the firm had to seek out a more gullible client base. My father's bank no doubt pocketed a fat commission as a reward for abusing him to serve its own ends.

I let loose an angry tirade. "How many times have I said that one should never buy anything that's being sold by Wall Street? *Never.* I like Moody's business, not their ratings. They always lag the market." As I spoke, it felt as if my throat was burning.

My father wanted to know if he should get rid of the bonds, which were now being quoted at around 34 cents on the dollar. "Yes," I said. "Sell them now." But it turned out that there was no liquidity at all, and his order was never executed. A few days later, on September 15, Lehman filed for Chapter 11. It was the biggest bankruptcy in US history.

I felt angry and humiliated. A big part of my identity is wrapped up in an image of myself as the protector and builder of wealth for my family and friends. I'd failed, and I was hurt that my father had inadvertently disempowered me by neglecting to inform me before he bought the bonds. But this wasn't just a blow to my ego. It also rattled me because it made me wonder what else I didn't know and what other chinks there were in my armor.

I had assumed that my defenses were totally solid, but I was starting to sense that this wasn't the case. For one thing, my father was easily the largest investor in my fund. The fact that he had been duped into buying Lehman bonds could have a serious knock-on effect. With the market crashing, I had a long-awaited opportunity to be a dispassionate buyer of companies whose shares had plunged to ridiculously low prices. I knew that I had to pick my spots, but I had spent enough time studying economic history and investors like Buffett to know that this might well be the best time in my entire life to buy stocks.

To do this, I needed my investors—especially my father—to stay calm during the storm. If his liquid assets were getting eroded, it would be that much harder for me to go against the crowd and continue buying while almost everyone else was in a panic. Knowing that my shareholders were facing these emotional and financial pressures placed an additional mental burden on me at a moment when I needed to be icily analytical.

The pressure intensified in other ways that I could never have predicted. For example, at the time, I employed a bright, hard-working equity analyst whom I regarded as a dependable ally. Then, one day in the fall of 2008, he came into my office, which I had come to think of as my bunker, and told me that he'd sold all of the stocks in his personal brokerage account. "I've gone to cash," he said. "I'm going to wait till things settle down and the outlook is clearer."

I was stunned. "Are you out of your mind?" I asked, unable to conceal my disgust. Here was a guy who had proudly claimed to be a value investor and whom I was paying to be rational. He was supposed to be a like-minded soul, helping me to seize these incredible opportunities that the market was gifting us. Yet his emotions were so out of control that even he was getting swept up in the panic. He just couldn't take it anymore. This is a measure of how acute the stress can become at a time like this—even for an intelligent and level-headed analyst who had previously come up with some highly profitable investments for the fund.

I would later decide never to hire another analyst, preferring not to expose my own mind to these insidious distortions. As usual, I should have done a better job of cloning Warren and Mohnish, neither of whom employed a full-time analyst. Needless to say, they were both buying cheap assets hand over fist at precisely the moment when weaker-minded investors were seeking the emotional comfort of cash.

As the global financial crisis deepened, the turmoil was unbelievable. Yet the bursting of the housing bubble was hardly a surprise to me. A few years earlier, I had paid close attention when Buffett explained at a Berkshire annual meeting why he no longer owned Freddie Mac: he and Munger had spotted the early warning signals when lending standards and accounting disclosures began to deteriorate beyond their comfort level. I had also read some brilliant investment letters by the hedge fund manager Michael Burry in which he cogently explained why there would be a disaster in housing and related financial markets. This is an important benefit of remaining in the right intellectual environment: clearheaded investors like Einhorn, Buffett, Munger, and Burry had helped to keep my eyes wide open.

As a result, I steered well away from the greatest danger areas. I shunned all housing-related businesses, including any company that financed them. Instead, my fund owned things like gas pipeline companies, which were about as far away from housing as I could get. Drilling for shale gas was a big growth market, and pipelines provided the cheapest mode of transportation from the gas fields to end users.

I did own some financial stocks, but I was certain that they were safe and had access to the liquidity they needed. For example, Master-Card didn't participate directly in the capital markets, and it provided one of the two dominant payment systems in the world. The closest my portfolio got to the epicenter of the crisis was Moody's, which had rated instruments that helped to fuel it. But Moody's balance sheet wasn't at risk; it was merely issuing an opinion about the credit worthiness of different companies rather than providing a guarantee. And there were plenty of precedents to show that they couldn't be held liable for expressing an opinion.

I had worked hard to invest in companies that sold for significantly less than their intrinsic value. All of them had high-quality moats, and they were all prodigious cash generators. None were highly leveraged or needed regular access to capital markets. The credit crisis was dangerous for any company that was leveraged and needed continuous access to money, whereas the long-term health of my companies looked remarkably sound. So when I first heard the news that Lehman was imploding and that liquidity was drying up, it seemed like a non-issue.

But it turned out that there was really no place to hide, especially for a long-only investor with a concentrated portfolio like mine, which consisted of around 15 stocks. I had successfully piloted the Aquamarine Fund through a number of previous market corrections, including the Asian crisis of 1997, the dot-com crash of 1999–2000, and the market jitters that followed September 11, 2001. In the fund's first ten years, I had substantially beaten the indexes, quadrupling the money of my original investors. My worst year ever had been a 6.7 percent loss in 1999.

But 2008 was something else. I'd never experienced an avalanche like this within my portfolio. The serious damage began in June when the fund fell by 11.8 percent. The following month, I was down another 3.5 percent. And then things started to get really ugly. In September, the fund fell by 6.8 percent; in October, it plunged by 20.3 percent; and in November, it tumbled by another 12.5 percent. For the year as a whole, I was down 46.7 percent. On paper, almost half of my shareholders' money and my family's money had gone up in smoke.

In the past, I had explicitly warned in my letters to shareholders that it was a statistical certainty that the fund would one day fall by as much as 50 percent. You only had to look at the tumultuous history of financial markets to know that this would eventually happen. The difficulty, of course, is predicting when these avalanches will occur. As a long-term investor, my choice—then and now—is not to attempt to time the market, which strikes me as an impossible task, at least for me. I also chose not to buy insurance (for example, by shorting an index or buying puts) since this reduces volatility but lowers your long-term rate of return.

For my temperament, this approach works. Emotionally, 2008 was painful for me. But I could deal with these massive paper losses because I understood that they didn't reflect the intrinsic value of my investments. I knew that I'd be fine if I made it through to the other side without being forced to fold by external forces. At some level, I was also making a macroeconomic call that we weren't heading into a repeat of the Great Depression since we had policymakers who understood the risks and were willing to use every available tool to avert disaster.

It also helped that I had prepared myself for precisely this sort of turmoil. One of the key financial decisions I had made as an adult was that I would never live beyond my means or fall into debt. The most I've ever owed is a few thousand dollars on my credit cards, which I've always repaid promptly. I've never leased a car or taken out a mortgage to buy a house. In 2008, when the market imploded, I was renting an apartment and had enough cash set aside to ride out the storm.

This attitude toward money is deeply embedded in my family's psyche. After fleeing from Nazi Germany in 1936, my grandfather used all of the savings he could take with him—a total of £1,000 in British currency—to build a house in Israel without borrowing a penny. When my parents moved our family to England in 1977, they bought a house in a less-expensive area of London than they could afford. And when I bought a place in upstate New York, I did it with cash, not debt. My wealthy ancestors had lost their fortune when they were forced to escape from Germany; at some deep-seated level, I live in mortal fear of this happening again. Understanding that this is an integral part of my wiring, I knew that I needed to avoid debt since it would interfere with my ability to act rationally. Likewise, I don't invest borrowed money because this added stress would make it impossible for me to remain calm and clearheaded.

My attitude toward debt had also been influenced by Warren Buffett—even before he told us the story of Rick Guerin's painful experience with leverage. At one point, Warren had a mortgage on his home in Omaha, but he's long since paid it off. In the past, he has also said that he never wants to get into serious debt because he doesn't want to discover how he's capable of behaving. I mentioned to him during our lunch that, when I was growing up in Israel, my parents couldn't afford to take us on vacation or buy a TV. They would wait patiently until they could afford what they wanted instead of borrowing to buy it. Occasionally, for a treat, we would go for iced coffee at an elegant hotel, the Dan Accadia in Herzliya. It was an inexpensive and prudent way to live the good life.

From a societal point of view, debt is a vital economic lubricant. Used in moderation, it's positively healthy. But for an individual investor, debt can be disastrous, making it even harder to stay in the game—both financially and emotionally—when the market turns against you. As Buffett wrote in his 2001 Letter to Shareholders, "You only find out who is swimming naked when the tide goes out." One of my shareholders was a third-party marketer who had previously persuaded me to travel with her to Europe for dog-and-pony shows designed to attract new investors to my fund. She was so keen on the fund's long-term value approach that she'd invested $2 million in it herself. But her faith in long-term investing suddenly disintegrated, and she cashed out in January 2009. I was flabbergasted. It wasn't clear if she couldn't bear the pain or if she was desperate for cash because she simply couldn't afford the losses we were suffering. What was clear was that her despair was an almost perfect signal that we had reached the point of maximum pessimism. A few months later, the markets bottomed and began to climb.

All but one of my institutional investors also bailed out, partly because they had a need for liquidity themselves. Still, the vast majority of my shareholders stayed firm, trusting that things would turn around. Most important, my father—who had faced life-threatening dangers as an Israeli soldier—remained extraordinarily calm. At the height of the crisis, when nearly half of his life savings had been vaporized, he asked me if he should withdraw some money from the fund. I said it was the worst possible moment to sell stocks, and I told him that I'd rather live in a shack than take any cash off the table.

To his eternal credit, he didn't withdraw a dime, even though he could have yanked out his money at short notice. His stake was large enough that he could effectively have shut down my business. But he never lost confidence in me. In retrospect, I realize that I was standing on the shoulders of a giant. Without his strength as a silent partner, I wouldn't have succeeded.

For fund managers, this whole issue of shareholder redemptions can be fraught with stress and difficulty. Before the crisis, my fund had about $120 million in assets under management. The market crash had slashed this to barely $60 million. To make matters worse, shareholders redeemed around $10 million more. One reason was that my fund's 90-day notice period made it a relatively easy asset to liquidate. Some other hedge funds actually suspended redemptions, taking advantage of self-serving clauses buried deep inside their offering documents by shrewd lawyers. I found this unconscionable.

To meet my investors' redemption requests, I had to be a net seller of stocks in an environment where they had never looked so cheap. By bailing out at this inopportune moment, a small minority of my investors made it far more difficult for me to act rationally and take advantage of these bargains. Instead, I had to allocate mental energy to the inordinately difficult task of deciding what to sell.

This taught me an important lesson. At that moment, what I most envied about Buffett was not his prodigious intelligence, but his structural advantage: he had permanent capital to invest since Berkshire is a company, not a fund. This meant that he didn't have to worry at all about how to meet shareholder redemptions. As a result, he was free to make enormous investments in equities at the perfect moment. According to Warren, temperament is more important than IQ when it comes to investing. This is no doubt true. But I'm convinced that having a structural advantage is even more important.

As for Mohnish, he had set up his fund so that investors could redeem shares only once a year. His investment losses in the market meltdown were even worse than mine. But he had to deal with redemption requests only once during the financial crisis, at the end of 2008. This structural advantage gave him more latitude than I had to think clearly about his portfolio. By contrast, the majority of my investors still owned a share class that allowed them to redeem quarterly. Ten years had passed since I founded the fund with this structure; now, after all this time, I was paying the price for my mistake. It was a potent reminder of how important it is to create the right structure from the very beginning.

In the midst of the crisis, I also envied Warren for his physical detachment from Wall Street and the investment herd. Unlike most professional investors, he seemed perfectly insulated from the fear and irrationality that had gripped the market. His small low-key office in Omaha is located in Kiewit Plaza, which he shares with the Kiewit Corporation, a contractor that builds infrastructure such as roads, bridges, and tunnels. It's an ideal spot for a contrarian investor to think dispassionately about where the crowd might be going wrong.

My own office—in Manhattan's Carnegie Hall Tower—was a terrible place to be in the midst of a financial crash. New York was at the heart of the crisis. And the building itself was filled with fearful investment professionals, including many hedge fund managers who were getting clobbered. Every morning I'd take a bus to work, no longer feeling that I should blow a few dollars on a cab. I would pass through the glass doors into the building's impressive lobby, which exudes an atmosphere of understated opulence. When I'd first moved into this skyscraper, I had felt like a Wall Street king. But now, it felt more as if I were entering a hospital. The faces all around me were drawn and pensive. This might sound overstated, but these expressions reminded me most of the looks I had seen on people's faces as they walked uptown through Manhattan on 9/11.

When I reached my office on the 25th floor, the mood was grim. In those brutal months, my employees were quieter and more serious than usual. There was no cheery banter. Nobody wanted to talk. While nothing was explicitly mentioned, they were clearly worried about their paychecks, and they were all dusting off their résumés. In the past, I'd mostly kept the door to my corner office ajar. Increasingly, I now closed it behind me, consciously trying to keep the outside world at bay so that this palpable gloom didn't infect my thinking.

Looking back now on the financial crisis, I'm pleased at how well I kept my emotions in check. By then, I had a sufficiently strong emotional core that I didn't get swept away by all of these intense pressures. It also helped that I was a true believer in the enduring power of value investing. This approach had worked for me for a decade, and I had absolutely no doubt that it would continue to work for me over the long term—if only I could stay the course.

Still, it wasn't easy to remain calm and positive. One way that I coped with the stress was to apply a strategy I had learned from Tony Robbins: studying heroes of mine who had successfully handled adversity, then imagining that they were by my side so that I could model their attitudes and behavior. One historical figure I used in this way was the Roman emperor and Stoic philosopher Marcus Aurelius. At night, I read excerpts from his *Meditations*. He wrote of the need to welcome adversity with gratitude as an opportunity to prove one's courage, fortitude, and resilience. I found this particularly helpful at a time when I couldn't allow myself to become fearful.

I also tried to imagine how Sir Ernest Shackleton would have felt in my shoes. He had made grievous mistakes on his great expedition to Antarctica—for example, failing to land his ship, *Endurance,* when he could and then abandoning his first camp too soon. Yet he succeeded in putting these errors behind him, and he ultimately saved the lives of everyone on his team. This helped me to realize that my own mistakes were an acceptable part of the process. Indeed, how could I possibly pilot the wealth of my friends and family without making mistakes or encountering the occasional storm? Like Shackleton, I needed to see that all was not lost and to retain my belief that I would make it through to the other side.

With this support from the eminent dead, I managed to keep my wits about me. I quietly went over my portfolio again and again, double- and triple-checking to be sure that my holdings had the wherewithal to survive. Confident of my analysis, I refused to sell a single share of major investments such as American Express. By March 2009, its stock had plummeted to around $10. I held on and rode it to a ninefold gain in the years that followed.

Only one of my holdings seemed too risky to keep: CarMax, a seller of secondhand vehicles. Its stock had already halved, but I was worried that the business model might be broken, given how difficult it had become for car buyers to obtain low-cost financing. Ultimately, I was proved wrong, and even CarMax bounced back. In this case alone, I had allowed the fears of the market to affect my rational thinking. It was a healthy reminder that I'm not immune to irrational fears, however carefully I try to guard against them.

At the same time, I was also buying some incredibly cheap stocks, despite the burden of meeting shareholder redemptions. For example, I invested in London Mining PLC, which was selling at a discount to the value of its cash. I loaded up on Brookfield Office Properties, which owned prime real estate that was being valued at way below its replacement cost. I bought stock in Cresud, an Argentinean owner of large tracts of valuable farmland, which I was getting for free since the whole company was selling for less than the value of its stake in IRSA, a publicly traded real estate firm. I also invested in Fortescue Metals Group, which had developed exceptionally low-cost reserves of seaborne iron ore. The price of iron ore had collapsed, but I was certain that Chinese demand would continue to grow.

These were elegant ideas. Not only were they remarkably cheap, but they each had catalysts that would inevitably emerge. Also, they didn't just have powerful earnings engines but also substantial collateral value. So the odds of success were exceptionally high.

All of these investment ideas emerged from conversations that I had with Mohnish, and I benefited immeasurably from his analytical brilliance. His thoughts and insights came at me thick and fast, and I was sometimes slow on the uptake. Mohnish joked that I seemed to be "drinking from a fire hydrant." Our growing friendship was one of the most precious rewards of the Buffett lunch, since that rich experience drew Mohnish and me so much closer together. I was amazed by his generosity in sharing his unconventional wisdom with me, and it's hard to do justice to his importance in helping me to make the right investments throughout the credit crisis.

All in all, it was like shooting fish in a barrel. Over the next few years, as the global economy recovered and normality slowly returned, every one of these stocks soared. For example, Brookfield doubled, Cresud tripled, and London Mining quadrupled. As I had thought at the time, the financial crisis may well have been a once-in-lifetime opportunity.

On the investing front, I'd acquitted myself well. My core stock-picking process was good. But I could see that there were still fundamental things that I needed to change about how I ran the fund and, for that matter, how I ran my life. The financial crisis had shown me that investment success isn't just a matter of identifying great stock ideas. As I had learned through painful experience, I also had to create the best possible environment for myself—physically, intellectually, and emotionally—so that I could operate more effectively and make myself less vulnerable to the sort of negative influences I'd encountered during the financial crisis.

Like Warren and Mohnish, I needed to be more strategic in the way I constructed this environment. I couldn't clone their intelligence, but I could see with increasing clarity that I needed to clone the aspects of their environment that had given them such a structural advantage.

So I decided to hit the reset button. Among the biggest changes I would make: leaving New York for Zurich in the summer of 2009.

8

MY OWN VERSION
OF OMAHA

Creating the Ideal Environment

ONE OF THE BIGGEST CHALLENGES FOR ANY INVES-
tor is that there are so many forces that mess with our minds. We like
to think of ourselves as rational creatures—which, to some extent, we
are—but the truth is a little murkier. The financial crisis had dem-
onstrated with brutal efficiency just how irrational investors can be,
especially in extreme situations.

The so-called professionals—myself included—are by no means
immune to these mind-warping distortions. I had witnessed this firsthand as my equity analyst, my institutional investors, and my third-
party marketer all cracked amid the pressure of a market crash, cashing
out at precisely the moment when they should have been buying. It's
reassuring to talk smugly about the "madness of crowds," but what
about the madness of the intellectual and financial elite? In my experience, we are capable of the same insanity. Indeed, it's often people of
my ilk who are driving the craziness.

The mind itself is a confounded thing, woefully ill-suited to the
task of investing. This is not a science book or a weighty tome about

the structure of the brain, but it's worth taking a few moments to ponder why it's so hard to think and invest in a rational manner.

People often misguidedly regard the brain as one structure: a neocortex that rationally takes in information, computes it, and spits out the answer. Daniel Kahneman, a trailblazing psychologist who won a Nobel Prize for economics in 2002, describes this aspect of the brain's processes with the phrase "thinking slow." For my part, I used to have a deluded image of myself as the equivalent of a fighter pilot, intensely focusing on the instrument panel in the cockpit of my jet, making optimal decisions and operating in full control of all the aircraft's levers.

Much of what we do at fine universities is intended to develop this rational, higher-thinking aspect of our minds. My friend Ken Shubin Stein teaches an advanced investment class at Columbia Business School. It's a phenomenal course that provides an enormous amount of useful insight into the investment research process. But all this learning and analysis is based upon the assumption that, when students graduate, it will be their rational neocortex that makes the investment decisions. The problem is that there is also a subrational, instinctive part of the brain—which Kahneman describes with the phrase "thinking fast"—where much of our decision making actually takes place.

Of course, I'm grossly oversimplifying an endlessly rich subject. If you'd like to research this further, you can read more lucid explanations by people like Kahneman, Dan Ariely, Jason Zweig, Joseph LeDoux, and Antonio Damasio. Reading works by these and other experts on behavioral finance and neuroeconomics, I became fascinated by the quirks and complexities of our decision-making processes. For example, the neurologist Benjamin Libet showed how a decision to take an action originates in the brain before the subject is aware that a decision has been made. Then there was the famous nineteenth-century case of Phineas Gage, who had suffered an accident that interfered with only one part of his brain; he appeared to function normally, but he was unable to make rational decisions.

I was also intrigued by research showing how the brain deals with signals that arrive at different times: the sight of a person's lip movements arrives instantaneously, while the sound they make arrives later, yet we perceive that these signals occur simultaneously. In other words, our brain constructs our reality, and it may not be doing so in an accurate manner.

Research of this kind helped me to see that the brain is a much less wieldy tool than we'd like to imagine. For participants in the stock market, one of the biggest problems is that the subrational, instinctive part of the brain is subject to dire mood swings, including outbreaks of irrational optimism and irrational pessimism. Indeed, money-related issues often activate the "subrational" parts of our brains. In situations of heightened financial risk, when we feel that we are in jeopardy, our subconscious instincts are activated; the neocortex can subsequently rationalize our decisions.

To understand who we really are as humans (and investors), it also helps to consider the environment in which we evolved. Roughly speaking, anatomically modern humans with large brains have been around for about 200,000 years. The part of our brain that evolved most recently is the rational neocortex. But for much of our history, we operated in a dramatically different environment. Today there are substantial parts of our mental apparatus that evolved to help us survive in the wilderness that was home to our hunter-gatherer ancestors. These primitive survival routines embedded in our brains are easily capable of bypassing the neocortex.

We might like to perceive ourselves as potential Isaac Newtons, but it's perilous to forget that we also have this other aspect of our nature. Indeed, Newton himself would have been better off if he'd recognized this, given that he was an infamously dumb investor who lost his life savings in the South Sea Bubble. As Newton wryly observed: "I can calculate the movement of stars, but not the madness of men."

The problem is not just that our brains are highly irrational. It's also that the economic universe operates in ways that are mind-blowingly complicated. The elegant economic theories that I learned at Oxford and Harvard blinded me to this awesome complexity. A few years after I started investing, the money manager Nick Sleep introduced me to the Santa Fe Institute, a transdisciplinary research community. I knew that Bill Miller, a remarkably smart fund manager at Legg Mason, was on the institute's board. So I started reading some of its research papers.

The key idea that I learned is to think of the economy as a complex adaptive system. Economists hate this notion because we can't model a complex adaptive system or use the type of math we've been trained to deploy. We also tend to be drawn to attractive, harmonious, hard-to-learn ideas such as the general equilibrium theory. This theory provides a wonderful account of how the world *ought* to work, and it can be a useful guide for policy makers. But it distorts our perception of reality.

Polymath investors like Bill Miller and Charlie Munger were quick to recognize that these standard economic models of the world are inadequate when it comes to the markets—and to see that models derived from biology may work better. Inspired by the Santa Fe Institute, I read *Journey to the Ants* by Bert Hölldobler and Edward O. Wilson. Much of the book is devoted to describing the different survival strategies used by ant species and to exploring how these different species have coevolved and competed with each other. This one book taught me more about economics than I'd learned in all my years at university. That may sound nuts, but it's true. Why? Because an ant colony, like the economy, is a complex adaptive system. Reading about ants was a revelation. For example, it turns out that ant colonies operate by a simple set of basic rules that enable them to resolve a myriad of difficult survival problems.

I realized instantly that I was discovering models that would be useful for me in analyzing the financial and economic world. My thoughts went to Munger and his latticework of mental models. So I sent him a copy of *Journey to the Ants*. To my delight, he replied with a short handwritten note, saying that he had long intended to read the book. Meanwhile, I resolved to spend more time reading books about biology. These studies deepened my sense that it's helpful to think of the economy as an evolving and infinitely complex biological eco- system. Companies, like ant species, must adopt strategies that enable them to thrive or they will be at risk of extinction.

As I soon discovered, other areas of complexity research also pro- vide helpful models for how the economic world operates. For exam- ple, the Danish theoretical physicist Per Bak coauthored a classic study of sandpiles that showed what happens when you keep dropping grains of sand in one area. The resulting pile reaches a state of "self-organized criticality"; avalanches then occur, but it's impossible to predict either their timing or their size. This model offers intriguing insights into market crashes, which have much in common with these avalanches. For investors, the bottom line is to avoid states of self-organized criti- cality, which is essentially what occurred in the stock market before the crash of 2008–2009.

The point is that the neat economic theories I had learned at uni- versity didn't come close to describing the true complexities of the economy or the financial markets. At the same time, I had also come to see that our brains are hopelessly limited in the face of this over- whelming complexity. This imbalance is a serious problem for inves- tors. Here we are—with our little irrational brains and our overly simplistic economic theories—somehow hoping to make sense of this unbelievably complex world. What chance do we have?

This isn't just a case of self-indulgent intellectual theorizing. It's a very real challenge for every investor. Is there any way, then, of tilt- ing the balance in our favor so that we increase the odds of victory in a game that's so heavily stacked against us? This is the question that underlies the next few chapters of this book.

In retrospect, I should have been far more skeptical about the eco- nomic models I had learned at university. So you'll be glad to hear that I'm not going to bore you with erudite discussions of the Black- Scholes model of option pricing, Keynesian macroeconomics and sticky prices, the IS/LM macroeconomic model, rational expectations, the Herfindahl industrial concentration ratio, or the Rüdiger Dornbusch exchange rate overshooting model.

This is, of course, sexy stuff that might serve you well if you're looking for love at a Mensa cocktail party or a gathering of central bankers. It might also get you a first-class degree and a great teaching gig. But in my experience, it's not particularly helpful when it comes to investing. The trouble is, economic theories like these tend to be based on intellectually elegant assumptions about how the world operates, not on the messy reality in which we actually live.

That said, there are plenty of useful things I learned at university that shouldn't be junked. For example, it's indispensable for any serious investor to know how to read a company's accounts. This doesn't mean simply grasping the difference between cash and accrual accounting. It also involves understanding the various ways that accounting rules can be used to skew the headline earnings numbers, not to mention the ability to tell whether the quality of earnings is increasing or decreasing. If you've picked up an MBA or a CFA, you've already gleaned the basic mechanics of this type of analysis. If not, there are lots of books that can impart this fundamental knowledge, including seminal works by Ben Graham and David Dodd, Marty Whitman, John Mihaljevic, Seth Klarman, and Joel Greenblatt. You don't need me to go over that well-trodden ground again.

Unfortunately, most investment books tend to focus on technical skills. It's fine to study basic concepts like return on investment, P/E ratios, and the like. But these things aren't hard, and they will get you only so far. Anyone who's smart enough to make it through business school can figure out how to dissect 10Ks, 10Qs, and other financial documents. The real challenge, in my view, is that the brain itself—which got us to where we are—is the weakest link. It's like a little boat, adrift in a sea of irrationality and subject to unexpected storms. And it's incompletely understood by even the most brilliant neuroscientists, let alone by investors.

When I started to read up on behavioral finance and neuroeconomics, there was a thrilling sense that I was fathoming some of the deepest mysteries of how the brain functions and malfunctions. But, initially, I mistakenly assumed that I could rely on my intellectual powers to overcome these irrational tendencies. As I read about the brain's shortcomings, I would nod knowingly, reassuring myself that I wouldn't trip up now that I had a better understanding of where these mental tripwires lay. But I gradually learned that intellectual knowledge and self-awareness are simply not enough. The difficulty is that we can't use the brain to override the brain. So we remain vulnerable to these mental shortcomings even when we know about them.

What, then, is the solution? This, I hope, is where I can help you by sharing what I've learned so far.

Through painful experience—both at D. H. Blair and in the financial crisis—I discovered that it's critical to banish the false assumption that I am truly capable of rational thought. Instead, I've found that one of my only advantages as an investor is the humble realization of just how flawed my brain really is. Once I accepted this, I could design an array of practical work-arounds based on my awareness of the minefield within my mind.

As it happens, this minefield may be particularly treacherous in my case. Around 2004, a friend who is on the faculty of the Mount Sinai School of Medicine sent me for an examination with his colleague Dr. Mary Solanto. She conducted a battery of tests and concluded that I have attention deficit disorder (ADD). The tests showed that I was capable of periods of extraordinary hyper-focus, especially at times of high stress, but that I was equally capable of falling through attention trapdoors when it came to the more mundane things in life. I could think great thoughts, but my attention could shift so easily that I had little grasp of basic things like what time it was or where I'd left my keys.

To deal with my ADD, I needed to develop an array of simple work-arounds—for example, installing big clocks in my office to help me keep track of time, having a clear desk so that I wouldn't get distracted, and putting objects in the same places so that I wouldn't lose them quite so often. In hiring a personal assistant, I specified that a key part of the job was to watch over me so that I wouldn't mess up simple tasks like catching flights, remembering appointments, or closing the front door when I left our office building.

All of this focus on building work-arounds and circuit breakers into my everyday life proved to be incredibly helpful—not just in dealing with my ADD but also in becoming a better investor. The truth is, all of us have mental shortcomings, though yours may be dramatically different from mine. With this in mind, I began to realize just how critical it is for investors to structure their environment to counter their mental weaknesses, idiosyncrasies, and irrational tendencies.

Following my move to Zurich, I focused tremendous energy on this task of creating the ideal environment in which to invest—one in which I'd be able to act slightly more rationally. The goal isn't to be smarter. It's to construct an environment in which my brain isn't subjected to quite such an extreme barrage of distractions and disturbing forces that can exacerbate my irrationality. For me, this has been a life-changing idea. I hope that I can do it justice here because it's radically improved my approach to investing, while also bringing me a happier and calmer life.

As we shall see in a later chapter, it wasn't just my environment that would change. I would also overhaul my basic habits and investment procedures to work around my irrationality. My brain would still be hopelessly imperfect. But these changes would subtly tilt the playing field to my advantage. To my mind, this is infinitely more helpful than focusing on things like analysts' quarterly earnings reports, Tobin's Q ratio, or pundits' useless market predictions—the sort of noise that preoccupies most investors.

The financial crisis had shown me beyond doubt that managing the nonrational part of my brain had to become an integral part of managing my stock portfolio. It also highlighted how hard it was for me to do this in Manhattan. We're all wired a little differently, but

New York—with its restless energy, competitive spirit, and pockets of extreme wealth—accentuated some aspects of my own irrational nature that aren't conducive to good investing. I needed to be in a place where I could think calmly and invest for the long term without the pressure of other people's expectations or the distraction of all the frenzied activity buffeting me in New York.

This is not to say that it isn't a fine base for some great investors. David Einhorn has thrived there; so have the managers of the Sequoia Fund. But I suspect that it's harder for people like me who flocked to New York from elsewhere and therefore lack the local roots that give emotional stability to people raised there. For outsiders, it's too easy to get unbalanced by the unbridled appetites—including greed and envy—that financial centers like New York and London can inflame.

To borrow a memorable term from Nassim Nicholas Taleb's book *The Black Swan: The Impact of the Highly Improbable,* these big cities are "Extremistan." As we know from various studies, the disparity between our own wealth and our neighbors' wealth can play a significant role in determining our happiness. If so, then reading about a New York–based multibillionaire like the Blackstone Group's Stephen Schwarzman may well trigger a destabilizing reaction in my irrational brain. Unless we have robust ways of dealing with these mind-bending forces, we can't avoid being knocked off course by them. For example, the proximity of so much extreme wealth might make it more tempting for me to swing for the fences with my investments instead of focusing calmly on making a decent compounded return without undue risk.

For me at least, it seemed wiser to live in a place where the differences are less extreme. Given my particular set of flaws and vulnerabilities, I figured that I would stand a better chance of operating somewhat rationally in the kind of place that Taleb describes as "Mediocristan," where life is more mundane.

So I started actively to consider alternatives to Manhattan. For a while, I thought seriously of moving to Omaha, given how well it had worked for Warren. I also considered Irvine, California, where Mohnish lives. I contemplated other American cities like Boston, Grand Rapids, and Boulder. And I thought about relatively low-key European cities such as Munich, Lyon, Nice, Geneva, and Oxford.

But in the end, Lory and I agreed on Zurich. I had gone there often as a child and had always liked it. More recently, I'd also read studies in which Zurich was routinely ranked as the world's leading city for quality of life. It wasn't hard to see why. It's a small, safe, manageable place with handsome architecture, clean air and water, and superb physical infrastructure. It has good public schools. There are beautiful mountains and great skiing just minutes away. It also has an excellent airport, easily accessible from the downtown area, with direct flights to places like New York, San Francisco, Singapore, Shanghai, and Sydney.

While Zurich is an expensive place to live, it's also highly egalitarian because everybody has access to more or less the same things—from pristine lakes to public swimming pools that are even better than the private one I'd enjoyed at our fancy country club in upstate New York. Likewise, Zurich's unsurpassed public transport system is so efficient that even local billionaires use it. The fact that the rich don't exist in an alternate reality that seems way out of reach for everyone else reduces the envy and the sense of lack that it's easy to feel in cities like New York and London.

I don't want to suggest that Zurich is perfect, but it has one other trait that seems remarkable to me: it's genuinely built on trust. For example, on the train system, tickets are seldom checked and there are no turnstiles. In stores, customers routinely buy wine and other products on credit and have them delivered to their homes, along with the invoice. Residents are part of a web of deserved trust, and this tends to bring out the best in them. In a way, this is a Buffettesque view of life. Warren treats the managers of his companies with considerable trust, granting them the latitude to make their own decisions, and they respond by doing everything they can to live up to his expectations.

Zurich also struck me as a place where I could live in mental peace—a quiet, pleasant, slightly bland setting where there isn't too much going on. Here I could focus on my family and my fund without undue disturbance. Occasionally people ask me, "But isn't it boring there?" My answer: "Boring is good. As an investor, that's exactly what I want." Because distraction is a real problem. What I really need is a plain, unobtrusive background that's not overly exciting. And I'm certainly not alone in finding Zurich conducive to clear thought. Historically, the city has provided a space for free contemplation to residents as diverse as Carl Jung, James Joyce, Richard Wagner, Vladimir Lenin, and Albert Einstein—not to mention Tina Turner.

It was also important that in Zurich I wouldn't be surrounded by people in the investment business. This would make it easier to go against the crowd without the risk that their thinking would seep into my own mind. Zurich is also far enough off the beaten track that not too many people would visit me; the friends and relatives who cared the most would come, but I wouldn't have to devote too much time to relationships that were less central to my life. This might sound cold and unsentimental, but these are the sort of things that I needed to consider as I constructed an environment that suited my idiosyncratic character and priorities. After all, in moving to Zurich I had a chance to start over with a clean slate, putting into practice all that I had learned about how I could function more effectively. I didn't want to blow it.

Next, I set about finding the perfect office—another key component of my new environment. Initially, I made a mistake, renting an office for a year on the Bahnhofstrasse, a ritzy street that is Zurich's own enclave of Extremistan. It's an elegant area, full of expensive stores. But super-rich settings like this are not ideal for me since they stimulate unhealthy appetites. So I soon decided to move to an office on the other side of the river, a 15-minute walk from the Bahnhof-strasse's glitz and glamour. For me, this feels like a safe distance.

The psychologist Roy Baumeister has shown that willpower is a limited resource, so we have to be careful not to deplete it. In fact, his lab discovered that even the simple act of resisting chocolate chip cookies left people with less willpower to perform subsequent tasks. In my case, I don't want to waste my limited energy guarding myself against the envy and greed that a place like the Bahnhofstrasse might trigger in me. It's better simply to construct my environment so that I'm not exposed to these destabilizing forces, which are likely to inten-sify my irrationality. The key is to free my mind from any unnecessary mental effort so I can use it for more constructive tasks that are likely to benefit me and my shareholders.

As I pondered these issues, I also began to recognize that other investors I admire had adopted a similar approach to building their en-vironment, whether consciously or not. Mohnish, for one, works in a less-than-glamorous office park in Southern California with no other financial institutions nearby. I once asked him why he hadn't set him-self up in an attractive office in one of Irvine's fancy shopping centers, close to his favorite restaurants. "Oh, Guy," he replied. "I don't need all that razzmatazz!" I have no doubt that he understands what the area around him can do to his mind.

Likewise, Seth Klarman, one of the most successful investors on the planet, works out of a decidedly unflashy office in Boston, far from the intoxications of Wall Street. If he wanted, he could easily rent the top floor of a gleaming skyscraper overlooking the Charles River. Nick Sleep set up his office in London near a Cornish pasty shop on the King's Road, far from the grandeur of Mayfair, which has become Britain's hedge fund mecca. Allen Benello, the manager of White River Investment Partners, works out of a nondescript office in San Francisco, nowhere near the city's financial district. And Buffett, as we've discussed, is tucked away in Omaha's Kiewit Plaza—another building that is not exactly known for its razzmatazz.

This strikes me as a significant yet largely unrecognized factor in the success of these investors. Small wonder, then, that I wanted to create my own version of Omaha.

That said, I'm different from Buffett—and not just in terms of IQ points. For one thing, it's important for me to have a pleasant view from my office, whereas he's not fussed about such aesthetic considerations. While I like to look out on trees or something similarly cheering, he routinely keeps the blinds drawn in his office. But in other substantive ways, I consciously modeled the environment he'd created in Omaha. For example, Warren lives about a ten-minute drive from his office, which is slightly outside the city center. Mohnish's office in Irvine is also about ten minutes from his home, and it's slightly outside the city center. I mirrored them, selecting an office that's a twelve-minute walk or seven-minute tram ride from my home and that's slightly outside the city center. For me, it works to be outside the heart of the city, partly because this makes it less likely that too many people will drop by the office opportunistically. They need a stronger reason to make this effort, so their visits tend to be more worthwhile.

These decisions were carefully considered. For example, Mohnish and I had specifically discussed commuting times, reaching the conclusion that the ideal commute takes around ten to twenty minutes. This is close enough to improve one's quality of life, but far enough to establish a separation between work and home. For people like me who get obsessive about their jobs, it's useful to have this separation. We need to see our families and spend time at home when we're not just buried in work. For the same reason, it's important to have hobbies. Among other things, I run and ski, which not only makes me healthier and happier, but clears my mind and strengthens my detachment from the mood swings of the market. If I spent that time holed up in my office, single-mindedly analyzing stocks, I'm certain that my decision making and my investment returns would suffer, along with my health and my family life.

In any case, everything is interconnected. My original motivation for creating a better environment had been to boost my returns. But these decisions also led to a better life.

Within the office itself, I was equally careful to construct an environment that would help me to operate rationally and effectively despite my balky wiring. Once again, it helps to know thyself—and to adapt thy setting accordingly. As I've mentioned, one of my flaws is that I'm amazingly easy to distract, and I need to address this problem in designing my physical environment. Unlike Buffett, who can operate brilliantly without a computer or an email address, I rely on my computer. But I'm also aware that the Internet and email can become appalling distractions for me. To counteract this and to help me remain focused, I physically divided my office.

At one end of the corridor, I have a "busy room," with a phone, a computer, and four monitors. But I keep the computer and the monitors on an adjustable-height desk, which I typically position so that I have to stand beside it. Responding to emails is a low mental task, but it's easy to get sucked into it for long stretches of time. So I've intentionally set up the desk in a way that prevents me from sitting at it. This might seem perverse, but the goal is to create an office that gives me the space to think quietly and calmly. Minor adjustments like this awkward positioning of the computer help to stack the odds in my favor.

At the other end of the corridor, I have a room that I call the library. Here, there's no phone or computer. I want to encourage myself to spend more time sitting and thinking, so this room is designed to be warm and welcoming. I can take piles of financial documents to study in there or select a book from the shelves that line the walls. If I close the door, it means that nobody is allowed to bother me. The library also serves as a nap room. Not coincidentally, Mohnish also naps in his office, and Warren told us that he has a place in his office where he can nap too. This isn't a matter of sloth—or, at least, not entirely! A daytime snooze keeps the mind fresh, shuts out the noise, and provides a chance to reboot the system.

Trivial as it might seem, even the way you decorate your office matters. Think of Oxford colleges, where the dining halls are adorned with portraits of illustrious alumni. On some level, their presence sends an inspiring message to the current flock of students. In a similar way, I positioned a bronze bust of Charlie Munger in my office. I'm not deifying him, but I want to activate his presence in my mind—not least as a cue to remind me of the dangers of those 24 forms of misjudgment that he identified in his talk at Harvard. Likewise, I keep photographs in my busy room and my library that show me with Warren and Mohnish on the day of our lunch.

I can't explain all of this on a rigorous scientific level. But my impression is that mirror neurons help us to model the influential people in our presence. By having images of Munger and Buffett in my office, I'm trying once again to tilt the playing field on a subconscious level, using their presence to influence my thoughts. My sense is that this is quite common. When I visited Winston Churchill's study at Chartwell, I was struck by the objects he kept on his desk, including a bust of Napoleon, a porcelain figurine of Admiral Nelson, and a photograph of the South African prime minister Jan Smuts. I don't think they were there merely for decoration. I'm guessing there were moments when Churchill would ask himself what these famous leaders would do in his situation. Religious objects such as crucifixes can presumably serve a similar purpose, providing a cue for the devout to improve their behavior. Given the power of mirroring, it's important to choose our heroes and role models with real care.

I also have photographs in my office of my father and some of my first investors, including a couple of his business partners. This is to remind me who I'm working for so that I never lose sight of my responsibility to my shareholders. Lately, I've been thinking of commissioning a single photographer to take black-and-white portraits of all my investors.

About a year after our charity lunch, Warren Buffett generously gave Mohnish and me an impromptu tour of his office in Omaha. I was fascinated to see how he had structured his own environment to enhance his ability to make rational decisions. Perhaps the most striking feature of his office was that it contained so little that could clutter his mind. He had only two chairs and no space for large meetings—a practical means of discouraging unnecessary interactions. His window shades were closed, presumably helping him to focus on the task at hand.

On the wall behind his desk, Warren had a prominently displayed photo of his father, Howard Buffett, whom he greatly admires. Lowenstein's biography of Warren describes Howard as an "unshakably ethical" Congressman who "refused offers of junkets and even turned down a part of his pay. During his first term, when the congressional salary was raised from $10,000 to $12,500, Howard left the extra money in the Capitol disbursement office, insisting that he had been elected at the lower salary." It's not hard to see this influence on Warren, whose modest salary for running Berkshire reflects a similar sense of integrity and altruism. More to the point, the photo is a reminder of how helpful it can be to include images of our role models when we are constructing our own work environment.

As for Warren's desk, it was so small that there was no room for piles, obliging him to process his reading efficiently. An in-box and an out-box lay on top of his desk, along with a box labeled "Too Hard"— a visual reminder that he should wait patiently until the perfect opportunity arrives. As he puts it, "I will only swing at pitches I really like." There's an element of playfulness about his "Too Hard" box, but its presence must also have a subtle effect on the way he thinks. These cues wouldn't help much if Buffett didn't also have an extraordinary mind. But it's interesting that even a man of his intelligence sees fit to keep that box on his desk as a physical aid that keeps his mind on track. To me, this shows a remarkable humility about his abilities.

I also found it telling that there was no Bloomberg terminal in Buffett's office. Apparently, there's one at the other end of the building, used by a Berkshire employee who manages a bond portfolio. Buffett could no doubt access it if he wanted to, but he's consciously chosen not to have this informational fire hose within easy reach.

Likewise, when I visited Nick Sleep's office in London, I was intrigued to discover that he kept his Bloomberg awkwardly positioned so that he could use it only while sitting on an uncomfortably low chair. Like Buffett, he had consciously designed his environment to discourage his use of a terminal that costs more than $20,000 a year to rent. Why? After all, a constant flow of information is surely the lifeblood of any professional investor.

My own relationship with the Bloomberg terminal is similarly ambivalent and tortured. It's a formidable tool, and there are times when I've found it helpful as a way to get stock data or news in a hurry. In my New York vortex years, my Bloomberg subscription also served the dubious purpose of bolstering my ego. It made me feel like a privileged member of a club that could afford the most expensive toys; without it, I might not have felt equal to my peer group. But beyond this foolishness, there's also a more serious downside to using a Bloomberg—or, for that matter, rival systems sold by companies like Reuters and FactSet.

All of these products—but especially the coveted, top-of-the-line Bloomberg—are ingeniously designed to lure the subscriber with the seductive promise of nonstop information. The terminal delivers such a relentless flood of news and data into investors' brains that it's hard to muster the self-discipline to turn off the spigot and concentrate on what matters most. You see stock tickers flashing before your eyes, news alerts blaring for your attention. Everything links to something else, so you often find yourself ricocheting into deeper and deeper recesses within this informational netherworld.

Initially, I was totally hooked. In my early years as a money manager, I would arrive in my Manhattan office and immediately fire up my Bloomberg. It would light up like a Christmas tree, its bright colors subconsciously spurring its users to action. But as I became more self-aware, I began to realize that this call to action wasn't helping me at all; nor were the endless hours of information surfing. I started to ask myself, "Is this really the best and highest use of my attention?" If I have only a limited amount of willpower, how much of it should I squander in trying to resist the temptation to snack on all of this informational sugar?

During the financial crisis, I saw more clearly than ever what an unhealthy addiction the Bloomberg had become. The constant barrage of bad news could easily have exacerbated my irrational tendencies, when what I needed most was to screen out the noise and focus on the long-term health of my portfolio. So I went cold turkey. In late 2008 and early 2009, as the market collapsed, I turned the monitor off for days on end. Another tactic that I used to distance myself from the Bloomberg was to stop having a personal login, though we still had a company login. I also changed the color scheme on my home screen so that it was dull and muted, thereby minimizing the risk that all those bright, flashing colors might jolt my irrational brain into unnecessary action.

In setting up my office in Zurich, I had to decide once again how to tackle the Bloomberg conundrum. By now, I was used to having the service. Psychologically, it would have been painful to let it go. I also knew that occasionally it was extraordinarily useful. But I was equally aware that, for me, it did more harm than good. So, in the end, I came to an uneasy compromise. I relegated the Bloomberg to the adjustable-height desk in my busy room. The fact that the desk is adjusted so that I usually have to stand means that there's little danger that I'll be tempted to use the Bloomberg for hours, grazing in a state of helpless distraction. Nowadays, I often go weeks without turning on the Bloomberg at all. Still, it's there if I ever need it—my own exceptionally expensive version of a toddler's security blanket.

Of course, the rational part of my brain tells me that I'd be better off getting rid of the Bloomberg entirely. Why bother paying more than $20,000 a year for a distraction that I can so easily do without? But I accept my fallibility. Instead of pretending to be perfectly rational, I find it more helpful to be honest with myself about my irrationality. At least then I can take practical steps that help me to manage my irrational self. Perhaps this is the best that any of us can do.

9

LEARNING TO
TAP DANCE

A New Sense of Playfulness

IN MOVING TO ZURICH, I DECIDED THAT I NEEDED TO change other aspects of my life too. It wasn't just a matter of constructing an environment that would help me to be more rational, less distracted, and calmer. I wanted to alter my attitude to life itself.

The experiences of 2008–2009 were so heightened and intense that it had been difficult for me to remain in balance. This is one of the biggest challenges for investors. We all know that it's important to be physically healthy, to have a satisfying personal life, and to maintain some kind of emotional equilibrium. But this holistic perspective is not just an airy-fairy, new-age dream: the truth is that it's hard to invest well if your non-investing life is out of whack, in chaos, or stunted.

Great investors don't often talk publicly about their emotional challenges. But George Soros gave some sense of the stresses of investing when he wrote that there were moments when he wasn't sure if he was running his fund or if his fund was running him. By contrast,

Buffett has said that he tap dances to work every morning. His playfulness and zest for life are reflected in his sense of humor and his love of bridge. He has found his passions, and he delights in them.

I wanted to inject more joy in my own life, to recapture the playfulness I had lost over the years. During the financial crisis, there were moments when my career seemed in real jeopardy. The market carnage was so extreme that countless funds went out of business. Even investors as famed as Bill Miller were mauled so badly that their reputations were severely damaged. One of the cleverest investors I knew, a guy from the year above me at Harvard, lost 80 percent and had to close his fund. He was still in his early 40s, but his once-glittering career as an investor was apparently finished. For me, the crash was the investing equivalent of a near-death experience. It forced me to reappraise how I wanted to live and what was truly important to me.

Amid this soul-searching, I began to see that I had locked myself into a view of my career as a life-or-death struggle. My approach was simply too extreme: I didn't just want to be a great investor, but to be Warren Buffett. For so many years, I had driven myself in an almost maniacally focused way to achieve my goals, acting as if my exam results, my university performance, and my fund's investment returns were everything, as if they defined who I was and determined my value.

Perhaps this stemmed from the ethos of my English education. At the age of 11, I had gone off to a British boarding school as an immigrant misfit who had already lived in Iran, Israel, and South Africa. Everything at school was a struggle for me, and I felt at the time that it was all about survival. In a sense, I carried this attitude blindly into my adult life, seeing my investing career as a kind of gladiatorial contest. In the wake of the financial crisis, I belatedly recognized that this tendency to approach life as a battle to the death was not necessarily useful, let alone a recipe for happiness.

I needed to lighten up. Figuratively at least, I wanted to learn to tap dance.

As part of this reinvention of myself, I was determined to have a lot more fun. One aspect of this was that I began to travel more. In 2009, for example, I took a ten-day trip to India with Mohnish. In the past, I would never have embarked on an adventure like this. I had felt obliged to work nonstop, so I would have convinced myself that I needed to stay home and watch over my stock portfolio. But I went to India with no agenda, and it turned out to be a marvelously enriching experience, helping me to see the world anew.

Among other things, I got to observe the remarkable work that Mohnish's Dakshana Foundation is doing to help educate kids on an industrial scale. It might sound like a platitude, but it also affected me deeply to see how happy many people were in India, despite having so little on a purely material level. It helped me to recognize how twisted our values can become in richer countries. And then there was the fascination of watching Mohnish in a nonprofessional setting, of seeing up close how he's wired. For me, there were lessons simply from observing his reaction to missed appointments and to people who behaved badly. I've seldom encountered anybody with his blend of calm and rational equanimity.

On that same trip, we also attended a TEDIndia conference in Mysore. I loved it. In the years that followed, I cofounded the TEDx-Zurich conference, attended events like the Art Basel show in Switzerland, and got more involved with supporting institutions such as Oxford, Harvard, and the Weizmann Institute of Science in Israel. I don't know if these things have made me a better investor, but they have certainly broadened my thinking, brought me many interesting relationships, and invigorated my life. Equally important, these activities are another aspect of being true to myself and who I am.

Meanwhile, in Zurich, I consciously avoided certain types of people. As I've mentioned, living in Switzerland and basing myself outside the city center made it harder for the "wrong" people to visit me. They needed a good reason to make the effort, and this acted as a useful filtering mechanism. Moving to Zurich also allowed me to cut through the

whole Gordian knot of my unhealthy relationships with fund marketers, equity analysts, and other professional "helpers" who had unhelp-
fully oriented me toward a standard, New-York-hedgie model of life.

But I wasn't looking to become a shut-in. On the contrary, I was
increasingly willing to invest large amounts of time and money to
travel anywhere to see people who were important to me. I went to
Israel with Ken Shubin Stein. I flew to California to spend a few days
with Mohnish, again with no agenda other than the pleasure of hanging out with a person I like and admire. Mohnish and I also set up a
mastermind group of eight people, the Latticework Club, which meets
every few months to share what's going on in our lives and to support
one another. This group has helped me to open up emotionally and to
introspect in a more systematic way.

For good measure, I also teamed up with my friend John Mihaljevic to create an annual event in Switzerland called VALUEx—a
community of like-minded people who share investment ideas and
wisdom while also forging friendships over meals and on the ski slopes
of Klosters. In 2014, more than 70 people flocked to Switzerland from
around the world to join us at VALUEx.

I had always enjoyed sports. But after moving to Zurich, I em-
braced them with more enthusiasm than ever. I ran or biked a few days
a week, and I took my kids skiing on weekends.

Likewise, I rediscovered my love of games, not least because the financial crisis had given me a renewed appreciation for how important
it is to be playful and not to take myself too seriously. I'd started to play
bridge around 2007, prompted by Mohnish, who is an ardent player,
and by the example of Buffett, Munger, and Bill Gates, all of whom
are bridge fanatics. Initially, I joined the Manhattan Bridge Club and
started taking lessons. Once I'd learned the basics, I quickly realized
that bridge was not only a pleasurable diversion but would help to
hone my skills in life, not to mention investing.

Indeed, as a preparation for investing, bridge is truly the ultimate
game. If I were putting together a curriculum on value investing,

bridge would undoubtedly be a part of it. As I began to discover the subtleties of the game, I was reminded of an intriguing comment that Charlie Munger had made about investing in his lecture on the causes of human misjudgment: "The right way to think is the way that Zeckhauser plays bridge. It's just that simple. And your brain doesn't naturally know how to think the way Zeckhauser knows how to play bridge." Richard Zeckhauser is a professor of political economy and a champion bridge player who chairs the Investment Decisions and Behavioral Finance Executive Program at Harvard. An expert on economic behavior in acutely uncertain situations, he has authored papers with titles like "Investing in the Unknown and Unknowable."

For investors, the beauty of bridge lies in the fact that it involves elements of chance, probabilistic thinking, and asymmetric information. When the cards are dealt, the only ones you can look at are your own. But as the cards are played, the probabilistic and asymmetric nature of the game becomes exquisite. For example, during the bidding, I might ask myself a question like this: "Given that the player to my right has bid two clubs, how does that update my probabilistic assessment of what cards he's holding?" As play continues, I might find myself thinking, "Aha, my partner has just led with the ace of spades. That must mean that she's also got a king or is short spades."

In investing, we constantly operate with limited information. For example, not so long ago, Mohnish and I researched a Chinese manufacturer of cars and batteries, BYD Auto. What initially triggered our interest was a story in the *Wall Street Journal,* which mentioned that Munger had liked the company and had spoken to Buffett about it. Warren then sent his top lieutenant at the time, David Sokol, to China. Shortly after that, Berkshire made an investment, and Sokol joined BYD's board.

As investors, we began to make probabilistic assessments about all of this public information. For example, we knew that Li Lu, who is Chinese-American, managed money for Munger. We had also read

Munger's public comment that BYD's CEO, Wang Chuan-Fu, "is a combination of Thomas Edison and Jack Welch—something like Edison in solving technical problems, and something like Welch in getting done what he needs to do. I have never seen anything like it."

In isolation, individual pieces of information like these don't count for that much. But they helped us to build a broader picture of what was going on and to update our knowledge of the company, prompting us to ask what Munger, Li Lu, Buffett, and Sokol might have seen in BYD that other investors had overlooked.

I remember talking with Mohnish at the time and expressing my skepticism about the stock, given that this Chinese company lay outside my circle of competence. In the end, it took me more than a year to get comfortable enough to invest with real confidence that I understood the business. Mohnish, a more adept bridge player and a less risk-averse investor, was able to buy earlier than me because he was comfortable with the inferences he could draw from partial information. As he put it to me, it counted for a lot to know that Buffett, Munger, Sokol, and Li Lu all considered the stock a winner. Mohnish's willingness to act on incomplete information enabled him to buy BYD at a much lower price than I paid once the information was more complete.

With my bridge hat on, I'm always searching for the underlying truth, based on insufficient information. The game has helped me to recognize that it's simply not possible to have a complete understanding of anything. We're never truly going to get to the bottom of what's going on inside a company, so we have to make probabilistic inferences.

This way of thinking proved particularly helpful after the credit crisis when almost everybody detested American money-center banks such as Citigroup, Bank of America, and JPMorgan Chase. I studied them carefully, asking myself bridge-like questions such as: "How on earth can I claim to understand the nuances of JPMorgan's $2 trillion balance sheet?" The answer: I couldn't. More important, neither could JPMorgan's own management—at least, not with great accuracy. But

I *could* make useful probabilistic inferences about the bank's balance sheets and earning power. I asked myself, "Going forward, are these likely to be better or worse than other investors expect?"

Meanwhile, I read in the news that Buffett had just made a $5 billion investment in the preferred stock of Bank of America. Based on probabilistic thinking, this suggested to me that he believed the Fed was committed to ensuring that money-center banks would be able to rebuild their balance sheets. Buffett's investment helped me to understand that the Fed was highly unlikely to raise interest rates until the banks were once again hugely profitable and healthy. For me, his weighing of these odds was revelatory. As Mohnish had pointed out, Buffett's involvement with banking stocks went back as far as 1969, and he'd almost never lost money on a bank bet. Given that nobody is a better investor in banks, Buffett's seal of approval meant a lot.

For good measure, at least half of Bank of America's rivals had fallen by the wayside, leaving the company in an even stronger position. Smaller banks would struggle to compete, given the mounting cost of technology in the banking sector. And the legal risks facing the bank seemed lower than most people realized: after all, the litigation over the Exxon Valdez oil spill is still going on after 25 years. So it seemed likely to us that the banking sector could drag out any lawsuits for many years, providing ample time to cover the potential cost of any claims.

I ended up investing heavily in an array of money-center banks whose stocks subsequently rebounded, much as Warren, Mohnish, and I had expected. My familiarity with bridge had helped me to become more adept at operating amid this kind of uncertainty. The key, perhaps, is that many investments are acutely uncertain, but not as risky as they might at first seem. People often assume that investors like me are great risk takers, perhaps little more than gamblers. Certainly, there are plenty of reckless investors with scant regard for the risk of loss, but they tend not to survive very long in the investing game. The long-term survivors possess a more sophisticated grasp of risk, including the ability to see when the situation is much less risky than the stock price might suggest. With JPMorgan Chase and the other money-center banks there was a lot of uncertainty, but very little risk.

Bridge wasn't the only game that captured my imagination or refined my mental habits. I also rediscovered the joys of chess, a wonderful game of analysis and pattern recognition. I first fell in love with chess at Harvard, thanks to my classmate Mark Pincus, who later founded Zynga, a social gaming company that made him a billionaire. Back in our student days, Mark noticed an unused chess set in my dorm and asked me to play. He thrashed me. I bought a stack of chess books and we continued to play. I gradually got better and started to win some games.

After graduating, I became a member of the Manhattan Chess Club and played pickup games in the park to escape from the horrors of my job at D. H. Blair. But my errant mind isn't quiet enough, so I've never become more than a half-decent player.

Back then, I had no sense of why chess was useful, not just enjoyable. But over the years, I've come to see that there are real tactical benefits to understanding how such games work. For example, in chess, there's a set repertoire of opening tricks and mistakes that lead unsuspecting players to a quick demise, usually within the first few moves. Initially, when I fell into these traps, I felt angry with my opponent. It seemed like an underhanded way to win. Then I'd become angry with myself for missing what's known as a "gotcha game." As I studied chess more, I became less prone to these basic mistakes.

There are useful parallels in the game of investing. For example, accounting is full of gotcha gambits. Corporations often manipulate accounting rules to present their numbers in deceptive ways—and the unsuspecting investor is easily duped into thinking that the situation is less dangerous than it really is.

In the late '90s, I analyzed a company that sold legal insurance. Like life insurance, this product was sold by brokers who received hefty commissions in return. The key to analyzing how profitable the firm really was lay in figuring out the correct rate at which to amortize the cost of acquiring its customers. This, in turn, was determined by how long those customers remained as clients after signing up. In my opinion, the company's accounts presented an overly sunny view of this, thus giving a misleading picture of the future. This struck me as the accounting equivalent of a gotcha game of chess. So I steered clear of the stock, which subsequently tumbled, triggering lawsuits and much hand-wringing among everyone except the short-sellers, who had bet against the company on the basis of this dubious accounting.

There was another way in which I found chess instructive. Early on, I had often found myself playing games against so-called duffers—a derisive term for players who make snap decisions based on emotions rather than on careful analysis. They either couldn't or wouldn't analyze the board in a considered manner. Initially, I often lost to the duffers. Their moves were so unpredictable that it would unnerve me and I'd lose my cool. But as I got better at the game, I became more disciplined, developing the mental fortitude to remain calm and careful even while my opponent played with wild abandon.

In the financial markets, plenty of investors—both amateur and professional—take foolhardy swings for the fences, betting on everything from hot tech stocks to overhyped IPOs. Sometimes these risky long shots pay off spectacularly, tempting other investors to follow their lead in making these duffer moves. But, as in chess, I've found that it ultimately works better to maintain my discipline and pursue a careful strategy with better odds of long-term success. In 2009, when many investors bailed out of stocks, they were once again making a classic duffer move. My opponent in that particular game wasn't an idiotic chess player but the madness of Mr. Market. I knew that I simply had to keep my cool and use this madness to my advantage by buying stocks that the duffers were selling.

I was also struck by the memorable mantra of a chess champion, Edward Lasker, who remarked, "When you see a good move, look for a better one." Applying this insight to stocks, I modified his mantra, often telling myself, "When you see a good investment, look for a better investment." Indeed, as Munger has pointed out, there's a common tendency to like a particular idea—whether it's a chess move or an investment—because it was the first one that popped into our heads. But is it really superior? Chess highlights the need to keep searching for a better move even after the brain has latched onto that first idea. Playing chess also strengthens this particular mental muscle.

At the same time, I drew another fundamental lesson from my amateur adventures in the world of bridge and chess. Yes, it's true that these games taught me helpful tactical lessons and mental habits while reinforcing my understanding of how critical it is to control my emotions. But these games also taught me a simpler truth: after so many years of taking life too seriously, I needed to adopt a more playful attitude. So instead of seeing everything—including my work—as a form of mortal combat, I began to approach it in a different spirit, as if it were a game.

I have no doubt that Mark Pincus had acted like this all along. As a lover of all sorts of games, he innately saw life as a game, and his playful attitude is an integral reason for his success. After Harvard, many of our classmates rushed to take dull positions at gold-standard investment banks and consulting firms. There was a common but shortsighted feeling that the first job out of school was a life-or-death decision. In reality, these first jobs are often all but irrelevant, given the direction that our careers later take.

While many of our classmates had sewn up their plum jobs as much as a year before graduating, Mark had no clear sense of what he'd do on leaving Harvard. He looked instead for companies that simply caught his interest, where he could keep playing the game of life. As a result, he went to work for John Malone at TCI in a suburb of Denver, learning lessons about the communications industry that later proved invaluable. The moment a more compelling opportunity arose, he left to found his first company. When I visited him in San Francisco in those early days, he told me, "It's not about how much money you make. It's about changing the world."

Steve Jobs took a similarly adventurous and playful approach to life. As he whimsically put it in his commencement speech at Stanford, "Stay foolish." Likewise, Buffett treats the investment business as a game and does little that compromises his day-to-day happiness.

After surviving the financial crisis, I became more conscious of the benefits of this lighter, more playful approach. Following Warren's lead, I stopped forcing myself to do things that I didn't want to do. To this day, I work hard, but I work my own hours; if I want to take a nap during the day, I take a nap. In 2009, my fund had a fantastic year, thanks in large part to the stocks I'd bought during the crash. One business associate told me that I should go out and market myself, pounding the table to get more people to invest with me. I told him, "I don't want to. I want to have a happy life. I don't need to have the biggest fund."

This attitude has undoubtedly made for a calmer and more joyful life. But I suspect it's also made me a better investor. To give you an analogy, when you drop a stone in a calm pond, you see the ripples. Likewise, in investing, if I want to see the big ideas, I need a peaceful and contented mind. This reminds me of a line that Mohnish often quotes from Blaise Pascal: "All of humanity's problems stem from man's inability to sit quietly in a room alone." Among the many gifts of my life in Zurich, none has been more important than my sense of quiet contentment. When I'm in this state, the right investment ideas have a way of bursting through to me. Surprisingly often, these ideas seize me while I'm on a bike ride or enjoying my life in some other way that's unconnected to the markets.

That said, some of my professional investor friends are bemused when they see me heading off on trips to India and the like. One of them chided me, "Guy, these things won't contribute to your returns." I had to explain that I was no longer trying to be the greatest investor at all costs. My goal is no longer to be Warren Buffett, even if I could be. My real mission is to be a more authentic version of myself.

At a recent annual meeting for my fund, someone in the audience asked me how I handle the process of selling stocks. I replied, "Badly." To some extent, I was being facetious. But I was also being light-heartedly honest because I don't believe that anyone handles the selling process particularly well. We can all claim to have clear rules—for example, declaring that a stock must be sold when it reaches 80 percent of its intrinsic value. But the truth is that this is an incredibly inexact science. There are stocks in my portfolio that, on a purely rational basis, I should probably sell. But I often hold onto them anyway. One reason is that I'm trying to manage myself, not just my portfolio. And I believe that my investment returns will be better over several decades if I master the trigger-happy side of my nature.

More to the point, in confessing publicly that I'm not particularly good at selling, I was no longer trying to dazzle anybody with my brilliance or convince people to invest in my fund. I was more focused on giving an honest account of myself than on selling. If people want to invest alongside me and my family, I'm delighted. If not, I no longer feel the stab of rejection that I felt in the past. After all, this is not life and death. It's not mortal combat.

But if I'm honest about it, there's still a deep-seated part of me that can never quite let go of the idea that money is a matter of survival. This is simply part of my wiring. Intellectually, I see the abundant benefits of viewing the stock market as a game—and I've no doubt improved as an investor by taking this more playful approach. But I also know that my shareholders' life savings are on the line. So investing may be a game, but for me, it's a deadly serious game.

10

INVESTING TOOLS

Building a Better Process

IF ANTS CAN USE A HANDFUL OF SIMPLE RULES TO DE-
velop an infinitely complex survival strategy, what about investors?
Can we create a similarly robust set of rules that will make our investment decisions smarter and less vulnerable to the distortions of our
irrational brains?

Here's one way to think about this: the human brain is said to run
on about 12 watts—in other words, only a fifth of the power that's
needed by a 60-watt light bulb. That's not much at all, given the power
consumption of some of the computers that exist today. Yet we expect
this relatively puny hardware to make immensely complex calculations
about the investing world, and we even have the audacity to hope that
we might get these calculations right.

As we've discussed, one way to tilt the playing field to our advantage is to construct an environment in which we can operate more
rationally—or at least less irrationally. But there's also another tool at
our disposal: if we're looking to make better investment decisions, it
helps immeasurably to develop a series of rules and routines that we
can apply consistently.

In the aftermath of the financial crisis, I worked hard to establish for myself this more structured approach to investing, thereby bringing more order and predictability to my behavior while also reducing the complexity of my decision-making process. Simplifying everything makes sense, given the brain's limited processing power. The rules that I developed encompass a wide-ranging assortment of critical investment processes, including what I read (and in what order) when I'm researching stocks; whom I speak with (and refuse to speak with) about potential investments; how I deal with corporate management; how I trade stocks; and how I communicate (and don't) with my shareholders.

Some of these rules are broadly applicable; others are more idiosyncratic and may work better for me than for you. What's more, this remains a work in progress—a game plan that I keep revising as I learn from experience what works best. Still, I'm convinced that it will help you enormously if you start thinking about your own investment processes in this structured, systematic way. Pilots internalize an explicit set of rules and procedures that guide their every action and ensure the safety of themselves and their passengers. Investors who are serious about achieving good returns without undue risk should follow their example. Why? Because in investing, as in flying, human error can be a bitch.

Like so many things in my investing life, my understanding of this issue grew out of conversations with Mohnish. During our trip to India in 2009, I quizzed him about all manner of things, including his approach to trading stocks. It was clear that he'd thought through these questions in a relentlessly logical way and constructed rules that governed everything he did. For example, as we'll discuss, he had decided that he'd never put in an order to buy or sell a stock during the hours when the market is open.

When I returned from that trip, I said to myself, "Guy, you're doing this all wrong." Mohnish is wired differently from me in many ways, including a readiness to assume more apparent risk—or uncertainty—than I'm willing or able to deal with emotionally. But I was determined to follow his lead in bringing this analytical rigor to my own process. Here, then, are eight of the rules, routines, and habits that I've subsequently put in place. This isn't an exhaustive list by any means. But I hope it gives you a flavor of what I've learned so far.

1. Stop Checking the Stock Price

When I settled in Zurich, I made a conscious decision to keep renting a Bloomberg terminal but not to switch it on when I got to work each morning. As I've mentioned, I now keep the Bloomberg switched off for weeks on end. But this is just one aspect of my effort to detach myself from the daily noise of the marketplace.

Many investors check their stock prices not only on a daily basis but also sometimes minute-by-minute. There's a peculiar glitch in our brains that somehow makes us think that the stock knows we're watching it. We may even have a nagging fear that if we stop paying constant attention, something bad will happen. Maybe a big news story will sideswipe us while we're not watching and the stock will suddenly blow up. Seeing the stock price on the monitor gives the investor a false measure of reassurance that everything is okay, that the earth is still revolving in its usual orbit.

The problem is, the constant movement of the stock price is a call to action. If I see a brightly lit ticker symbol flashing on my Bloomberg screen, it tells my irrational brain that I need to do something. If you're speculating on the latest hot biotech or Internet stock, it may make some sense to follow every mad gyration: a brokerage firm issues a wildly bullish report and your stock suddenly surges by 20 percent as other speculators pile in. But I'm trying to invest in a more measured way, buying stakes in companies that I'm looking to hold for years, if not indefinitely. As Buffett has said, when we invest in a business, we should be willing to own it even if the stock market were to close the next day and not reopen for five years.

I can't switch off my monitor for five years because I need to approve the net asset value of my fund once a month so that I can send a monthly update to my shareholders on the value of their stake in our partnership. But if I were managing solely my own account, I'd set up a system in which I'd look at the price of my holdings only once a quarter, or possibly even once a year. As things stand, I check the price of my holdings no more than once a week. It's a wonderful release to see that your portfolio does just fine when you don't check it. For good measure, I don't have my computer or Bloomberg monitor set up to show me the price of *all* my holdings on one screen; if I need to check the price of a stock, I do it individually so that I won't see the price of all my other stocks at the same time. I don't want to see these other prices unnecessarily and to subject myself to this barrage of calls to action.

It's worth thinking a little more about the effect of all this gratuitous noise on my poor brain. Checking the stock price too frequently uses up my limited willpower since it requires me to expend unnecessary mental energy simply resisting these calls to action. Given that my mental energy is a scarce resource, I want to direct it in more constructive ways.

We also know from behavioral finance research by Daniel Kahneman and Amos Tversky that investors feel the pain of loss twice as acutely as the pleasure of gain. So I need to protect my brain from the emotional storm that occurs when I see that my stocks—or the market—are down. If there's average volatility, the market is typically up in most years over a 20-year period. But if I check it frequently, there's a much higher probability that it will be down at that particular moment. (Nassim Taleb explains this in detail in his superb book *Fooled by Randomness*.) Why, then, put myself in a position where I may have a negative emotional reaction to this short-term drop, which sends all the wrong signals to my brain?

In any case, with the type of businesses I invest in, it's not imperative to know what's going on from day to day. Virtually all my investments are in companies where the long-term outcome is all but inexorable: the company is heading in that positive direction, and it's really just a question of how long it takes. Buffett's holdings clearly possess this same precious characteristic. Indeed, he uses the word "inevitable" to describe the positive outcome that he ultimately expects. Consider his stake in Burlington Northern Santa Fe. There's no question that its transportation network will become more valuable as the US economy grows, the country becomes more built up, and the railway industry consolidates. Plus, nobody will build a rival railway track next door, so Burlington won't be displaced.

If you invest in businesses like this that are truly inexorable, it shouldn't really matter if you switch off the monitor, curl up on the sofa, and read a book. After all, Buffett didn't make billions off companies like American Express and Coca-Cola by focusing on the meaningless daily movements of the stock ticker.

The Rule: Check stock prices as infrequently as possible.

2. If Someone Tries to Sell You Something, Don't Buy It

In the early years of my New York vortex period, my fund's returns were decent, and I was hurt that nobody seemed to be paying attention to me. Then I must have landed on various databases because the phone started ringing off the hook. Everybody wanted to sell me something. Brokers rang to pitch me stocks. Sales reps called to sell me high-priced research systems, investment newsletter subscriptions, new phone services, and countless other products. At first, these calls seemed a measure of my success, as if all this attention put me on the map. But I soon began to see that I made lousy decisions when I bought things that salespeople were hawking to me.

The problem is that my brain (and most likely your brain too) is awful at making rational decisions when confronted with a well-argued, detailed pitch from a gifted salesperson. So I adopted a simple rule that has proved extraordinarily beneficial. When people call to pitch me anything at all, I reply in as pleasant a manner as possible, "I'm sorry. But I have a rule that I don't allow myself to buy anything that's being sold to me."

Aghast, salespeople counter with questions like: "But how are you going to pick the right phone service?" Sell-side equity analysts opine: "But don't you think this is a great stock?"

Sometimes they're no doubt right. Logically, perhaps, I *should* switch phone services or load up on their brilliant investment idea. But I just won't do it. I may miss out in the short term. But over a lifetime I have no doubt that I'll benefit much more by detaching myself from people with a self-interest in getting me to buy stuff. This is a simple application of "adverse selection." As Charlie Munger has joked, "All I want to know is where I'm going to die so I'll never go there." For me, if an investment is being sold, that's a place where I certainly want to avoid going.

I even apply this rule if I'm at a cocktail party and someone starts telling me about a great stock they own or a private company in which they'd like me to invest. I may listen. I may be impressed. I may even be tempted. But I won't buy it if they would gain something from my doing so. In some cases, this might not be a sales commission or any other financial benefit: it might simply be that they derive psychological validation from successfully selling their idea. Either way, this is a no-go zone for me because the provenance of the idea is wrong since it stems from the seller's personal agenda.

As usual, Buffett knew this long before I did. For example, he has a rule never to participate in an open outcry auction. Following his lead, I've never invested in an IPO and probably never will. When a company is going public, it has all of the mind-warping sales power of Wall Street behind it. Of course, some IPOs catch the wind perfectly and soar. But the provenance is toxic, so it's safer for me to cross all

IPOs off my buy list, even if this means missing out on an occasional winner.

The Rule: If the seller has a self-interest in me buying, I ain't buying.

3. Don't Talk to Management

For much the same reason, I don't want to speak with the management of the companies I'm researching. Many smart investors would disagree with me on this. For them, it's possible that regular contact with senior executives may be fruitful. Also, this promise of high-level access can be a useful marketing tool, appealing to existing shareholders and prospective investors who may not understand that talking to management has a potential downside.

Heretical as this might sound, my own experience is that close contact with management is more likely to be detrimental to my investment returns. The trouble is, senior managers—particularly CEOs—tend to be highly skilled salespeople. No matter how their business is performing, they have a gift for making the listener feel optimistic about the company's prospects. This ability to win over their audience, including board members and shareholders, may be the most important talent that got them to the top of the corporate food chain. But this gift of the gab doesn't necessarily make them a dependable source of information.

This isn't to say that CEOs, CFOs, and other top executives are malicious or immoral. Far be it from me to suggest anything so disrespectful! It's just that their job, their agenda, and their skills lead them to present information in a way that accentuates the positive while discounting any business problems by describing them as either temporary or solvable. They may be skewing information subconsciously, without any bad intent. But it doesn't matter. Knowing my own rational limitations, I'd prefer not to expose myself to this potentially distorting influence. And it strikes me as especially dangerous for investors to allow management to help form their *first* impressions of a company.

I know some money managers who will do their research, then say, "I need to meet management so I can get comfortable." But who knows how management will mess with their minds? If I have to meet the CEO to understand why I should buy the stock, that's a serious warning sign. It should be clear enough from all of my other research. And if I want to assess the quality of the management, I'd rather do it in a detached and impersonal way by studying the annual reports and other public data, along with news stories. It's better to observe them indirectly like this instead of venturing into their distortion field by meeting them one-on-one.

In retrospect, I realize that it was observing Mohnish that convinced me to stop speaking with management. When we first discussed this around 2008, it was a foreign concept to me since it flew in the face of conventional wisdom, even among value investors. Now I wonder why it took me so long to understand that this simple practice cuts out a whole lot of noise.

The Rule: Beware of CEOs and other top management, no matter how charismatic, persuasive, and amiable they seem.

Exceptions to the rule: Berkshire's chairman and CEO, Warren E. Buffett, and a small but growing minority of CEOs (at companies like Fairfax Financial, Leucadia National Corporation, and Markel Insurance) who take seriously the idea of sharing what *they* would like to know if they were in their shareholders' shoes.

4. Gather Investment Research in the Right Order

We know from Munger's speech on the causes of human misjudgment that the first idea to enter the brain tends to be the one that sticks. As he explained, "the human mind is a lot like the human egg, and the human egg has a shut-off device. When one sperm gets in, it shuts down so the next one can't get in. The human mind has a big tendency of the same sort." If that's true, I need to be extremely careful about the order in which I gather research and explore investment ideas. I want to evaluate them from a position of strength, not weakness. If the idea comes from a salesperson, it immediately puts me in a weak position. So, as we've discussed, I simply eliminate ideas from salespeople: I don't want to allow a sell-side analyst's pitch (however well-reasoned) to be the first idea that settles insidiously inside my brain.

But what if a friend or peer I respect suggests that I look at a particular stock that they think I should buy? Even hearing about an idea verbally like this isn't ideal because it's difficult for any investor to be detached and rational when a smart person tells them why something is great. So I try to stop them short and say something like, "Wow, it sounds really interesting. Let me read up on it before we talk so we can have an informed conversation about it."

If I have a business relationship with the person, I can tell them, "I'd love to hear about your investment idea. Please could you send it to me in writing?" If they object and say, "Oh, but I really need to talk to you about it first," I tell them that I just can't do it. Socially, it might seem awkward to insist on getting an idea in writing first. But it's important to take as much heat and emotion as possible out of the research process. In my experience, I'm much better at filtering what I read than what I hear.

Once I decide that an investment idea is promising enough for me to explore it further, I still need to be careful to do the research in the right sequence. This might not seem important to many investors, but the order in which I read the materials matters greatly since whatever I take in first will affect me unduly.

My routine is to start with the least biased and most objective sources. These are typically the company's public filings, including the annual report, 10K, 10Q, and proxy statement. These aren't perfect, but they are prepared with a good deal of care and attention, especially in the United States, and they are reviewed by lawyers. The company doesn't want to get sued, so there's an incentive to produce financial statements that investors can rely upon. The accountant's audit letter is also key. Occasionally, accountants may be under intense pressure to sign off on the accounts, overlooking any irregularities. But the auditor's letter can subtly signal that the accounts are not all that they appear to be. Reading financial statements is more of an art than a science. Even if it's not explicit, you sometimes sense that management is trying to provide less information than investors might find useful. As in poker, unconscious "tells" can appear even in a footnote, making you wonder if something is amiss.

In the annual report, the management's introductory letter is also important. Is it a public relations puff piece, or is there a genuine desire to communicate what's going on? I want to avoid promotional companies that are bent on showing things in the best possible light. By contrast, when Berkshire released the offering document for its B-class shares, it candidly stated that Warren and Charlie wouldn't buy them at that price.

After working my way through the corporate filings, I typically turn to less objective corporate documents—things like earnings announcements, press releases, and transcripts of conference calls. There might also be helpful information to glean from a book about the company or its founder. These are fairly useful if they're not just vanity pieces since many hours of work have gone into them; in some cases, they have such depth that I'd read them before the corporate filings. Investors looking at Berkshire for the first time would do well to read the books that Roger Lowenstein and Alice Schroeder wrote about Buffett. Likewise, in studying Wal-Mart, a good place to start would be Sam Walton's book *Made in America*.

These ideas about the sequencing of information may seem trite. But minor shifts in how we operate can have a major impact. By consistently improving the way I consume information, I'm looking to create better conditions for success over many years. Still, we're all wired differently, so my idea of a healthy and balanced informational diet may be different from yours. The *Wall Street Journal* once noted that Buffett had a small TV in his office, tuned to CNBC, but with the volume muted. I'd find it terribly distracting to have a TV at work as it would stimulate my brain in unhelpful ways.

I also try (and sometimes fail) to minimize my exposure to the Internet, which can lead me in a thousand different directions. It requires a lot of mental energy to read a web page, with all its links to other information. I don't want my mind's chain to be yanked. So I prefer to read the physical editions of things like the *Wall Street Journal,* the *Financial Times,* the *Economist, Barron's, Fortune, Bloomberg Businessweek,* and *Forbes,* along with more abstruse publications like *American Banker* and the *International Railway Journal.*

Still, I avoid reading any press coverage until after I've studied the corporate filings. There are plenty of good journalists who provide useful context and insight. But for my purposes, it's important not to prioritize news stories, since they give my brain reasons to act, often without providing real substance. The corporate filings are my meat and vegetables—less enjoyable, but usually more nutritious.

As for the equity research published by brokerage firms, I read little of it, and I never rely on it. Once I'm finished with all of my other research, I sometimes pull up these reports so that I know what Wall Street is saying about a company or industry. But I'm careful to make this research the last thing I read, so that I've already formed my own impression. I don't deny that there are smart people working on the sell side. In some cases, they provide remarkable insight, particularly about industry dynamics. So it would be unwise and unfair to dismiss an entire community. But their work is paid for by brokerage dollars. When I read it, I'm exposing myself to Wall Street, which is one big selling machine. Also, my goal in creating all of these habits is to get out of sync with the markets; moving in lockstep with them is a recipe for average results.

The Rule: Pay attention to the order in which you consume information. And don't eat your dessert until you've finished your meat and vegetables.

5. Discuss Your Investment Ideas Only with People Who Have No Axe to Grind

By now I probably sound like some weird mix of social outcast and appalling snob—refusing to speak with CEOs, sell-side analysts, or anyone else from the world of sales. Many of them are no doubt charming, upstanding citizens with mortgages to pay and angelic children to support. But, in my eyes, their underlying sales agenda is a fatal flaw. So is there anyone that I am actually happy to speak with about potential investments? Good question. Thanks for asking.

If I want somebody else's perspective (and I often do), I find it more useful to seek out the opinion of a trusted peer on the buy side. Over the years, I've had invaluable discussions with investors like Nick Sleep, Chris Hohn, Bill Ackman, Steven Wallman, Allen Benello, Ken Shubin Stein, Dante Albertini, Jonathan Brandt, and Greg Alexander. All of them have taught me a great deal without trying to teach me anything. In my experience, the best people to speak with about investments aren't just intelligent but have an ability to keep their ego out of the conversation. As a result, these discussions tend to be playful and fun, and they don't disturb my calm pond. Increasingly, the person I speak with most about potential investments is Mohnish, partly because his analytical gifts are off the charts, but also because he doesn't have any axe to grind.

I've found that investment discussions work best when they adhere to three ground rules that I borrowed from groups like the Young Presidents' Organization. First, the conversation must be strictly confidential. Second, neither person can tell the other what to do as this tends to make people feel judged, so they become defensive. In fact, it helps if you don't even know whether the other person is thinking of buying or selling the stock since that knowledge muddies the waters. Third, we can't have any business relationship because this could skew the conversation by adding a subtle or not-so-subtle financial agenda. Of course, what matters most in these conversations is mutual trust. So no action should be taken unless the other person gives clear permission. If I'm interested in buying the stock or discussing it with someone else, I need to ask specifically if that's okay. If it's not, I can't do it.

The goal of these conversations isn't to reach the "right answer" or engage in intelligent debate. It's to share our experiences and information. To achieve this, it helps to ask open-ended questions. For example, instead of asking what a company will earn next year, it's more useful to ask something like, "What needs to happen for them to generate a lot of cash next year?"

I remember a specific conversation that I had with Shai Dardashti, a money manager friend who has given me permission to share what we discussed. At the time, he was researching K-Swiss, a manufacturer of athletic shoes. I had done a lot of research into Nike and had looked at the impact of its sponsorship on tennis and soccer. Instead of telling Shai that I thought K-Swiss was an also-ran in the sneaker business, I suggested that he produce a list of the top 20 tennis players, see who sponsored them, then estimate which of those players attracted the most viewers in what is typically a winner-take-all market. In the process, he discovered that K-Swiss had only one player on the list, while Nike had six or seven—an indication that K-Swiss faced an all but insuperable challenge to win market share away from Nike. At no point did we discuss whether Shai already owned the stock or was thinking of buying it. But I'm guessing that our discussion helped to clarify that it wasn't the best place for him to invest.

The Rule: Pool your knowledge with other investors, but stick with people who can keep their ego in check. If the other person happens to be Buffett, Munger, or Pabrai, so much the better.

6. Never Buy or Sell Stocks When the Market Is Open

Wall Street is perfectly designed to take advantage of weaknesses in the human brain. For example, unscrupulous brokerages create well-honed scripts that enable their brokers to call their marks—I mean clients—to convince them to buy particular stocks. The underlying goal is to generate lucrative trading activity for the firm itself. As a long-term value investor, my interests are in stark opposition to the interests of Wall Street. What I need to do is simply invest in a handful of great but undervalued businesses and then stay put. Wall Street is rewarded for activity. My shareholders and I are rewarded for inactivity.

To help myself function this way, I need a series of circuit breakers that slow me down and prevent me from acting precipitously. Some of these routines and procedures are so obvious that it might seem as if they are not even worth mentioning. But I've found them immensely beneficial, and it doesn't take a lot of energy or thought to implement them.

When it comes to buying and selling stocks, I need to detach myself from the price action of the market, which can stir up my emotions, stimulate my desire to act, and cloud my judgment. So I have a rule, inspired by Mohnish, that I don't trade stocks while the market is open. Instead, I prefer to wait until trading hours have ended. I then email one of my two brokers—preferring not to speak with them directly—and ask to trade the stock at the average price for the upcoming day. I'm not trying to get an edge on the market because I don't want to get swept up in its constant mood swings. As Ben Graham explained, we have to try to make the market our servant, not our master.

Occasionally I break this rule because there's a particularly compelling reason to trade a stock during market hours. As with all of these rules, the point is not to let them become a straitjacket but to have them guide my behavior in a generally healthier direction. In the case of this trading rule, what matters is that I'm giving myself permission to disengage from the market.

By contrast, in my early years as a fund manager, I had an in-house trading desk. This was a terrible idea because it brought the market into the heart of my office in a way that was even worse than having a Bloomberg terminal. I also used to talk directly to traders, who would ask me questions like, "Do you want me to take a look on the floor and get some color on the market?" I didn't know any better so I let myself be exposed to this head-spinning barrage of market action. All this information made me feel powerful and gave me an illusion of control.

My view now is that we're simply not wired to deal with this constant flood of price information. But it took years for me to learn this and also to develop the discipline to say, "I'm just going to ignore all this noise." At first, this can be quite scary. But in my experience, it's marvelously liberating.

The Rule: Keep the market at a safe distance. Don't let it invade your office or your brain.

7. If a Stock Tumbles after You Buy It, Don't Sell It for Two Years

When a stock has surged, selling it can be a joy. But it can also be bittersweet, like parting with an old friend. When a stock has tumbled, selling it is even more emotionally fraught. After all, it's hard to make rational decisions about an investment that has already lost you a lot of money since negative emotions such as remorse, self-loathing, and fear can short-circuit the ability to think clearly. Mohnish developed a rule to deal with the psychological forces aroused in these situations: if he buys a stock and it goes down, he won't allow himself to sell it for two years.

He explained this to me around the time of our lunch with Warren Buffett, and it made so much sense that I instantly adopted this rule. Once again, it acts as a circuit breaker, a way to slow me down and improve my odds of making rational decisions. Even more important, it forces me to be more careful before buying a stock since I know that I'll have to live with my mistakes for at least two years. That knowledge helps me to avoid a lot of bad investments. In fact, before buying a stock, I consciously assume that the price will immediately fall by 50 percent, and I ask myself if I'll be able to live through it. I then buy only the amount that I could handle emotionally if this were to happen.

Mohnish's rule is a variation on an important idea that Warren has often shared with students. As Warren once put it, "I could improve your ultimate financial welfare by giving you a ticket with only 20 slots in it, so that you had 20 punches—representing investments that you got to make in a lifetime. And once you'd punched through the card, you couldn't make any more investments at all. Under those rules, you'd really think carefully about what you did, and you'd be forced to load up on what you'd really thought about. So you'd do much better."

The Rule: Before buying any stock, make sure you like it enough to hold on for at least two years, even if the price halves right after you buy it.

8. Don't Talk about Your Current Investments

Over the years, I began to realize that it was a bad idea to speak publicly about stocks that I own. The issue isn't that other investors might steal my best ideas. The real problem is that it messes with my head. Once we've made a public statement, it's psychologically difficult to back away from what we've said—even if we've come to regret that opinion. So the last thing I want to do is walk into the trap of making a public statement about a stock, given that the situation might later change or that I might subsequently discover that I was wrong.

I first encountered this idea in Munger's talk on the causes of human misjudgment, which led me to Robert Cialdini's book *Influence: Science and Practice.* Cialdini described this peculiar feature of our mental wiring as the "commitment and consistency principle." To demonstrate this idea, he wrote about a 1966 psychology experiment in which residents of Palo Alto were asked if they'd do something that wouldn't cost much money but would help their neighborhood. A few days later, they were asked to put an ugly sign on their front lawns to stop drivers speeding through the neighborhood. Residents who had previously committed to doing something inexpensive to help their neighborhood found it extraordinarily hard to change their stated position so they typically felt obliged to install these signs on their lawns.

Likewise, if you tell a child that you're going to give them a treat, they're liable to reply, "You promise?" They intuitively understand that you'll find it hard to reverse course after taking a position.

I experienced this firsthand with a stock called EVCI, which I bought around 2003. Within 18 months, it surged seven-fold, making it the most successful investment I had made up to that point. As we'll discuss later, I should have sold all of my shares. But I had given an interview to *Value Investor Insight*, extolling EVCI as an example of my investing prowess. As a result, I was publicly invested in the stock and couldn't part with it even though it was no longer cheap. For various reasons, the stock subsequently halved. In retrospect, I could see that I would have been much better off if I'd never spoken about it since this would have given me more latitude to sell once the circumstances changed.

Still, it took me a long time to act on this knowledge and actually stop speaking publicly about my holdings. Sometimes it was necessary to disclose what I was doing. For example, after my fund was battered in the financial crisis, I needed to reassure my shareholders so that they wouldn't lose heart. I talked to them at length about current holdings such as Cresud and London Mining, making it clear that these were remarkably cheap stocks with great prospects.

In 2010, after my fund had rebounded sharply, I finally made the change: I stopped discussing my current investments in public settings, including my annual meetings, interviews with journalists, and letters to shareholders. At first, this wasn't an easy shift to make. Once you create an expectation in the marketplace, it's difficult to reverse yourself without people feeling that they're being shortchanged. But this change in procedure was well worth the risk of leaving a few noses bent out of shape.

I'm not dogmatic about this rule. If I'm chatting privately with a shareholder, I might end up talking about a particular stock that we own. But even in these private conversations, I try to remain neutral and understated, resisting the temptation to talk heatedly about why I think a stock is great. I know how hard it can subsequently be to make a decision that's inconsistent with these statements. So why create this potential headache when it's so easily avoidable?

Instead of discussing current holdings in my letters to shareholders, I now provide a detailed postmortem on stocks that I've already sold. This gives shareholders a clear insight into how their money is being invested, but it doesn't interfere with my ability to act as rationally as possible going forward. For me, this has certainly removed a psychological burden. I'd argue that most individual investors would also benefit from keeping quiet about their current investments since this talk only makes it harder to operate in a rational way. It's so much easier when you don't have to worry about how other people might judge you.

The Rule: Don't say anything publicly about your investments that you may live to regret.

11

AN INVESTOR'S CHECKLIST

Survival Strategies from a Surgeon

EVEN WITH A WELL-CONSTRUCTED ENVIRONMENT and a robust set of investment rules, we're still going to mess up. The brain is simply not designed to work with meticulous logic through all of the possible outcomes of our investment decisions. The complexity of the business and economic world, combined with our irrationality in the face of money-related issues, guarantees that we'll make plenty of dumb mistakes. The habits and processes that we've discussed so far should help us to edge in the right direction. But there is one other investment tool that is so invaluable that it merits a chapter of its own: a checklist.

The goal in creating a checklist is to avoid obvious and predictable errors. Before I make the final decision to buy any stock, I turn to my checklist in a last-ditch effort to prevent my unreliable brain from overlooking any potential warning signs that I might have missed. The checklist is the final circuit breaker in my decision-making process.

The idea for this didn't originate with me, but with Atul Gawande. A former Rhodes Scholar at Oxford, he is now a surgeon at

Brigham and Women's Hospital in Boston, a professor of surgery at Harvard Medical School, and a renowned author. He's a remarkable blend of practitioner and thinker, and also an exceptionally nice guy.

In December 2007, Gawande published a story in *The New Yorker* entitled "The Checklist," which drew heavily on his experience as a surgeon to explore a problem that is both profound and practical. As he put it, "intensive-care medicine has grown so far beyond ordinary complexity that avoiding daily mistakes is proving impossible even for our super-specialists." As he explained, this reflects a fundamental challenge that exists in other fields, too—namely, "the art of managing extreme complexity," and the question of "whether such complexity can, in fact, be humanly mastered."

His article went on to describe the groundbreaking work of Peter Pronovost, a critical-care specialist at Johns Hopkins Hospital, who designed a checklist after a particular patient nearly died. Pronovost took a single sheet of paper and listed all of the steps required to avoid the infection that had almost killed the man. These steps were all "no-brainers," yet it turned out that doctors skipped at least one step with over a third of their patients. When the hospital began to use checklists, numerous deaths were prevented. This was partly because checklists helped with memory recall, "especially with mundane matters that are easily overlooked," and partly because they made explicit the importance of certain precautions. Other hospitals followed suit, adopting checklists as a pragmatic way of coping with complexity.

When Mohnish read Gawande's article, he had a eureka moment, instantly recognizing that the idea of a checklist could also be applied to investing—another field in which the complexity is so extreme that even super-specialists routinely trip up, making easily preventable mistakes. In our case, it isn't fatal. But investing errors can be terribly costly to shareholders with their life savings on the line.

I was sitting in my office in Manhattan one afternoon when Mohnish emailed me a copy of Gawande's article. We then spoke on the phone, and it was clear that he was really excited. Mohnish has the kind of mind that easily makes unusual connections, so it was immediately obvious to him that the checklist idea was a big deal. I thought it was interesting, but it took me longer to understand just how significant it might be. By now, I'm used to the fact that Mohnish is quicker on the uptake than I am. I console myself by contemplating a sage observation of Buffett's: "The key to life is figuring out who to be the batboy for." As I realized long ago, there's no dishonor in being Mohnish's batboy. Far from it. And while I'm busy cloning Mohnish Pabrai, he's busy cloning Atul Gawande.

Mohnish pursued the checklist idea with ferocious intensity and rigor. He began by marshaling a group of us to recall a slew of investing mistakes we had made. In each case, we had to work out why they had happened and if there was a cause that we should have seen beforehand. Sometimes I would look back at a situation where I had missed some vital clue, shake my head, and say, "How did I not see that?"

Mohnish added his own mistakes to the mix. We combined these with some (infrequent) errors that we had seen Buffett and Munger make, including their investments in NetJets, Dexter Shoe Company, and Diversified Retailing—a reminder that retail is a tougher place to make money than most people realize. Buffett, with characteristic candor, confessed in his 2007 letter to shareholders: "To date, Dexter is the worst deal I've made. But I'll make more mistakes in the future—you can bet on that. A line from Bobby Bare's country song explains what too often happens with acquisitions: 'I've never gone to bed with an ugly woman, but I've sure woke up with a few.'"

Mohnish and I also discussed Berkshire's ill-timed investment in CORT Furniture in 2000. CORT had made a fortune leasing furniture to start-up companies during the heady years of the 1990s tech boom. But Buffett and Munger had underestimated just how vulnerable its profits would be when this bubble burst. Companies like eBay and Craigslist also ate into CORT's sales by making it cheap and easy to buy used furniture. Munger later described this investment as a "macro-economic mistake."

I helped Mohnish by carefully analyzing my own errors, along with those of other investors. Mohnish himself worked at such a breakneck pace that it was almost unnerving. After we had compiled our initial list of mistakes—and the lessons we should draw from them—he hired a couple of graduate students from Harvard Business School to undertake a painstaking forensic investigation. They studied the 13F filings of about 20 smart value investors (including firms like Southeastern Asset Management and Fairholme Capital Management), counting as a mistake any investment they had sold at a loss. The students then read through the investors' public statements and annual letters to reconstruct the thinking behind these failed investments.

Gawande himself became intrigued by what we were doing. He interviewed Mohnish and me, and he wrote a few pages about us in his 2009 bestseller *The Checklist Manifesto: How to Get Things Right*. Among other things, he mentioned Mohnish's realization that he had "repeatedly erred" in underestimating the riskiness of leveraged companies. As I suggested to Gawande, part of the problem might lie in what I described as "cocaine brain": the intoxicating prospect of making money can arouse the same reward circuits in the brain that are stimulated by drugs, making the rational mind ignore supposedly extraneous details that are actually very relevant. Needless to say, this mental state is not the best condition in which to conduct a cool and dispassionate analysis of investment risk.

By the time I settled in Zurich, we had assembled a veritable cornucopia of cock-ups. These included several mistakes that Mohnish and I had made in the run-up to the credit crisis, when some of our stocks plunged by more than 80 percent. In our postmortem analysis, we were able to explore where we had gone wrong—and, more important, design checklist items that would help to prevent us from repeating these mistakes.

Mohnish, who did the lion's share of the work in this whole endeavor, ended up grouping his checklist into about six broader categories, including themes such as leverage and corporate management. It's an incredible piece of intellectual property. My own checklist, which borrows shamelessly from his, includes about 70 items, but it continues to evolve. Before pulling the trigger on any investment, I pull out the checklist from my computer or the filing cabinet near my desk to see what I might be missing. Sometimes, this takes me as little as 15 minutes, but it's led me to abandon literally dozens of investments that I might otherwise have made. In a typical case, I might conclude, "Okay, this stock is failing on four of my checklist items." On that basis, I'm unlikely to invest in it. But this isn't a black-and-white mechanical process.

As I've discovered from having ADD, the mind has a way of skipping over certain pieces of information—including rudimentary stuff like where I've left my keys. This also happens during the investment process. The checklist is invaluable because it redirects and challenges the investor's wandering attention in a systematic manner. I sometimes use my checklist in the middle of the investing process to deepen my understanding of a company, but it's most useful right at the end as a way of backstopping myself.

That said, it's important to recognize that my checklist should not be your checklist. This isn't something you can outsource since your checklist has to reflect your own unique experience, knowledge, and previous mistakes. It's critical to go through the arduous process of analyzing where things have gone wrong for you in the past so you can see if there are any recurring patterns or particular areas of vulnerability. We're all different, and we mess up in ways that are often quite personal to us. For example, some investors are temperamentally drawn to the opportunities available in highly leveraged companies. I'm not, so I don't need to have as many checklist items that warn me to tread carefully in this kind of risky environment. By contrast, Mohnish is less fearful of heavily indebted companies, so this is one area where he might need to be more cautious.

Similarly, an investor like Bill Ackman seems drawn to opportunities involving controversial stocks where the management may be bamboozling gullible investors. If I were Bill, I'd have a checklist item that said, "Am I being drawn into this situation not because it's the best investment I can make, but because I enjoy the thrill of the investigative chase and want to right the wrongs of the world?" This is not a criticism of Bill, who is a superb investor and would have made an equally outstanding investigative journalist. It's a matter of looking at our idiosyncrasies and understanding where they tend to lead us.

In my case, it's particularly important for me to feel that people like me; I also find it hard to say "no" to people I like. This makes me vulnerable in certain situations as these emotional needs could short-circuit my rational judgment. To help counter this, my checklist includes questions such as: "Is there some way in which this investment idea is being sold to me? Does someone in this situation have an axe to grind? Who benefits if I make this investment? Does this investment appeal to any personal biases of mine that should be reexamined?"

Given my nature, it makes sense to explore this question of whether I might be trying to fulfill some other part of my personality instead of just maximizing my returns. A checklist is a way of managing your own mind and guarding against your own proclivities, so it needs to be based on this kind of self-awareness.

My other caveat is that a checklist is emphatically not a shopping list of the desirable attributes that we're looking for in a business. I've seen investment checklists that ask questions like: "Is this company cheap?" Or: "Does it have a high return on equity?" In my opinion, this is a misguided way to use checklists. I prefer to use them in much the same way that pilots use them. They don't ask: "Does this plane fly fast?" Or: "Am I flying to a sunny destination?" Rather, the items on their checklists are designed to help them avoid mistakes that have previously led to plane crashes. In investing too, the real purpose of a checklist is to serve as a survival tool, based on the haunting remembrance of things past.

But the best way to explain this is to provide you with some real-world examples of how I developed my checklist. Here, then, are four brief case studies—situations in which I made costly investment errors that then led me to develop specific checklist items. The point is not just to relish this humbling account of various low points in my stock-picking career. It's to get a clearer sense of how you might analyze *your* mistakes and blind spots in order to construct a checklist of your own.

Case Study One: The Man Who Lost His Cool

Back in 2001, when I was living in Manhattan, I began to make an array of investments in companies that provided for-profit education. I traveled all over the world to learn more about these businesses, searching wide and deep for good companies in the same sector. I flew to Singapore, Shanghai, and Mumbai to research one of the global leaders, Raffles Education Corporation, and I dispatched my analyst to the Philippines. But it turned out that some of the most intriguing companies in the industry were in my own backyard. I put together a list of all the for-profit educational institutions in New York City and went door-to-door on my BMW motorcycle to check them out. At the time, I must have known more about the sector than almost any other investor in America. And I loved riding that bike!

During these visits, I came across an obscure college called Interboro Institute, which was owned by EVCI Career Holdings Corp. This company's enterprising management team had come up with an innovative way of providing a college education to students with limited resources, many of whom had failed to graduate from high school. The students typically received financial aid grants that exceeded the cost of Interboro's bare-bones education. So they were educated for free while EVCI made money in the process. This model later came under fire. But I attended at least three graduation ceremonies at Interboro and saw for myself that it provided real social value. Essentially, it helped less-than-stellar students to get a degree and move on to jobs in fields like medical billing and insurance administration instead of remaining in menial work such as packing groceries.

During the early stages of my research, I mentioned EVCI to Whitney Tilson, and we ended up visiting the company together in

Yonkers. The business was doing well, but EVCI was hobbled by $2 million in debt that it had issued to acquire Interboro. In June 2003, Whitney and I invested $1 million each in EVCI, which relieved the company of this debt burden and invigorated the business. Meanwhile, the number of students at Interboro grew rapidly, profits surged, and my $1 million investment soared to $7 million in 18 months.

This was part of the benefit of running a small fund like Aquamarine: I could take a meaningful position in a tiny company like this, which operated way below the radar of larger funds. It was thrilling, too, to see how my legwork had paid off. All in all, this investment felt like a triumph. I felt really proud. When a stock takes flight like this, there's a sense of joyous wonder: "Wow," you think. "That's real money."

With EVCI's operating income and stock both up seven-fold, the board agreed to grant huge pay rises to the company's two top executives. The chairman/CEO would see his base salary leap from $326,000 a year to $621,000, and the president's base salary would jump from $267,000 to $483,000. I was grateful for their astute management of the company up to that point, and I wanted them to get rich alongside their investors. But this was a miniscule company that had generated less than $3.5 million in operating profits the previous year. Their pay hike meant that these two executives would now take roughly a quarter of the operating profits in cash for themselves. To me and to other investors, that was an outrageous amount for a company of this size. After all, who owns the company? The management or the shareholders? In retrospect, I should have sold my shares right then.

I was shocked and upset. This struck me as a short-sighted and self-serving business decision, and I fired off a forthright letter to the management and the board, describing the compensation plan (somewhat tactlessly) as "inane" and complaining that it undermined investors' confidence in them. For a start, I explained, the plan was financially inefficient since a big slug of the profits would now go to the IRS to pay income taxes. Even worse, these hefty salaries would have to be declared in the company's proxy documents for all to read. Interboro's competitors were in the state sector, where educational administrators had no opportunity to earn that kind of money. I was worried that these inflated salaries would spark resentment, not least among New York State's education authorities. This could result in unwanted reviews of Interboro's business and possibly even a withdrawal of its education license.

My letter suggested what seemed to me a compelling alternative. I said I was willing to use my influence as a substantial shareholder to pass a compensation plan that would give the two top executives a generous grant of stock options. If the stock kept climbing, they could each make tens of millions of dollars. This struck me as a strong incentive and an appropriate reward for enriching their shareholders. But I received no reply from the management or the board of directors. I found this inexplicable. Here I was, offering to help them make a fortune. Yet they didn't even deign to respond.

Convinced that my arguments would win him over, I arranged to meet EVCI's chairman/CEO for lunch at a restaurant near his office in Yonkers. Our conversation seemed cordial until suddenly all hell broke loose. He began shouting at me at the top of his voice, and the whole restaurant fell into stunned silence. It felt like a scene from a movie. I don't remember his exact words, but I think he yelled, "Are you accusing me of lying?" He also said something to the effect of, "Who the hell do you think you are?"

I froze and had no idea how to react. I thought I was offering him an opportunity to make enormous sums. In return, he seemed determined to humiliate me publicly. This was an astounding turn of events. What I discovered much later was that he was going through a bitter divorce. According to a 2009 decision from the New York Court of Appeals, he and his wife were fighting over their marital assets, including his stock in EVCI. His wife commenced divorce proceedings in 2003, a trial ensued, and she was later granted a divorce on the grounds of abandonment. In 2006, the trial court "rejected" his "claims that the appreciation in the value of the EVCI stock was due solely to his efforts," and it used the trial date "for valuation purposes" of his stock and options.

In other words, he was in the midst of a wrenching war over money—and specifically over his stake in EVCI. This helps to explain why he blew up at me when I proposed that he reverse the decision to increase his salary and instead receive a massive payday only if the stock performed well. Perhaps, his concern was that a major portion of this future wealth might end up going to his ex-wife. In any event, he must have felt under attack from every side. And, of course, we know how difficult it is to act rationally when money is at stake. In my opinion, the chairman/CEO was a smart and decent person. But it seemed to me that he had landed in a difficult position that didn't bring out the best in him.

Our contentious lunch was an augury of more trouble to come. EVCI's stock soon halved—at which point, I finally sold my shares. As I had predicted, the company also lost favor with the state education authorities: in 2007 the New York Board of Regents enacted new test regulations that made it much harder for Interboro students to receive financial aid. The company was also ordered to repay millions of dollars in student-aid funds after it turned out that some of its students had been ineligible for the money they received. In December 2007 the *Chronicle of Higher Education* reported that EVCI had decided to close Interboro down "after it realized that most of its students would no longer qualify for state or federal student aid." The company was also hit with a class-action lawsuit for securities fraud. It was an ignominious end to what had once seemed an inspiring success story.

Later, when I performed a postmortem on my various investing mistakes, I reexamined what had happened at EVCI and tried to draw some practical lessons from the experience. For me, one of the most important was that I needed to be more conscious of the extent to which the life circumstances of top executives can affect their decision making and their ability to manage the business. If I have even a mild argument with my wife, it can put me out of sorts for the day, affecting both my mood and my ability to make intelligent decisions. So I can only imagine how hard it would be to go through a contentious divorce. Indeed, this is just one example of the many life events that can knock an executive off track: it might also be a family bereavement, a major dispute with a business partner, or even extreme levels of personal debt.

Life is messy, and we all go through trying times. But it's important to recognize that senior management—like the rest of us—can be derailed by this kind of personal turmoil. After all, when a person's back is up against the wall, it increases the likelihood that their judgment will suffer. So I added a couple of items to my checklist as a formal reminder of some hard-earned lessons, courtesy of this education company.

Checklist Items: Are any of the key members of the company's management team going through a difficult personal experience that might radically affect their ability to act for the benefit of their shareholders? Also, has this management team previously done anything self-serving that appears dumb?

Case Study Two: A Tortuous Tale of Tupperware

The Tupperware Plastics Company was founded in 1938 by Earl Silas Tupper, who had previously worked at DuPont Chemical. He fashioned Tupperware's first containers out of polyethylene slag, a waste product from oil refining. Today, his iconic brand of plastic containers is sold in about a hundred countries. Instead of selling these goods in stores, the company's strategy relies upon a legion of "consultants" who organize Tupperware "home parties," at which the host receives free items in return for inviting guests to see the product line.

Back in the late '90s, I became intrigued with Tupperware, which seemed to embody all of the attributes of a high-quality business. I was particularly impressed with its exceptional profit margins and return on equity. Here was a company that could take $5 worth of plastic and turn it into a piece of Tupperware that sold for $50. The company generated lots of cash, and it didn't need much capital. Plus, I remembered Munger talking about Tupperware parties in his lecture on human misjudgment. He said these parties exemplified an array of the "manipulative psychological tricks" that Robert Cialdini had discussed in his books. The overall effect was said to be so powerful that housewives bought masses of Tupperware despite its high price.

I wanted to experience this firsthand. So a friend and I hosted a Tupperware party in my apartment in New York. I was awed to see these psychological forces at play. For a start, there was the reciprocation principle. As the hosts, we knew that we'd get some free Tupperware, based on how much was sold at the party. So we were already grateful to the Tupperware lady for agreeing to organize the event, and we were excited about the free containers we'd receive as our reward. Then, at the start of the event, the Tupperware lady handed out a small gift to everyone so that none of our guests would leave empty-handed. The result: everybody at the party was itching to reciprocate, just as Cialdini would have predicted.

Another psychological force at play was the liking principle. We liked the friends we had invited, and they liked us. Once the Tupperware lady had handed out free gifts, we all liked her too. Half an hour earlier she had been a complete stranger; now she was not just a friend but a member of our team.

The list goes on. For example, the authority principle was also at work since she knew a remarkable amount about food, which enhanced her authority as a Tupperware salesperson. There was also a scarcity factor at play since she hadn't brought enough items to satisfy all of the demand among our guests. And did I mention that the Tupperware containers came in all these really bright, vivid colors that also caught our attention? In short, the party was a brilliant example of sales psychology at its most effective. In a couple of hours, our Tupperware lady sold more than $2,000 worth of the product, earning herself nearly $1,000.

Having seen this phenomenon in person, I felt that I understood why the company was so successful: its superior performance was based on the remarkable psychological effects unleashed at these parties. Plus, I could see that there was endless opportunity for Tupperware in emerging markets even though the developed world might already be saturated. Armed with these insights, I pretty much raced out to buy the stock. I was secure in the knowledge that every two minutes someone was hosting a Tupperware party somewhere in the world, and that these principles would be playing themselves out.

Sadly, I was wrong. While some investments fail quickly, this one failed slowly—and that can be far more damaging to an investment portfolio because these slow losers suck up an enormous amount of your mental energy over an extended period of time. For as long as I owned Tupperware, one region or another was always performing badly. Sales simply weren't growing. I would listen in on the company's quarterly conference calls to find out what was going wrong. These calls reassured me that management was highly competent and working hard. But as I gradually realized, the company faced a fundamental problem: there was too much competition, and the high price of its products had become a serious obstacle to growth.

It was only after a couple of years that I really figured out what was going on. When Tupperware first hit the market, its products were unique. Customers willingly paid a premium for its promise of "sealed-in freshness." But over the decades, many other competitors got into the game, and their seals improved until they were just as good. These rival products may not have been as attractive, but they were cheaper, and they were easily available in supermarkets. As a result, Tupperware could no longer justify its high price for a simple product. Despite the management team's abundant skills, they couldn't alter this harsh economic reality. As Buffett once remarked, "When a management team with a reputation for brilliance tackles a business with a reputation for bad economics, it is the reputation of the business that remains intact."

I finally capitulated in the summer of 1999, selling the stock for more or less what I had paid for it a couple of years earlier. Looking back on this disappointing investment, it was clear that I had failed to ask the most obvious question: does this product offer good value for money? After the positive experience of hosting a Tupperware party, I had become too committed psychologically to the idea of owning the stock, and I lacked the detachment to see the pitfalls.

This misadventure taught me an invaluable lesson: I want to invest only in companies that are a win-win for their entire ecosystem. In consultant speak, we'd refer to the ecosystem as "the value chain." The terminology doesn't matter. What's important is the idea that a great company makes tons of money while adding real value for its customers. Originally, Tupperware had done this by introducing an innovative product. Now, no more.

By contrast, consider a world-beating business like Wal-Mart (or, for that matter, Costco, GEICO, or Amazon.com). Wal-Mart works hard to make everything it sells less expensive for the consumer, constantly driving more costs out of its distribution system. This pleases its customers, so they bring more of their business to Wal-Mart each year. You might think that Wal-Mart's suppliers would be resentful since their margins are getting squeezed. But the suppliers benefit from the sheer volume of sales generated in Wal-Mart's stores. Everybody in this ecosystem wins: Wal-Mart and its shareholders, its suppliers, and its customers. (That said, I've never owned Wal-Mart since the company was already too large and the stock too expensive to meet my criteria. And, of course, Wal-Mart has critics who would argue that its success comes at the expense of local businesses and its own workforce.)

In future, I determined to do a better job of analyzing the whole value chain to identify companies that make it more efficient. This analysis would have saved me from my Tupperware mistake. It has also kept me away from companies as diverse as Philip Morris (a phenomenally profitable business that is damaging to its customers' health) and Greece's national lottery firm OPAP (a phenomenally profitable business that is damaging to its customers' wealth). Both of these companies have a license to print money. But they do so by preying on people's weaknesses. For the consumer and for society at large, this is not a win-win proposition.

Personally, I don't want to invest in companies that make society worse even if their products are legal. Call me irrational, but I think it's bad karma. In any case, I much prefer to invest in businesses that benefit society. Once again, in learning this lesson, I realized that Buffett already knew it; as far as I'm aware, every one of his holdings meets this high standard.

Checklist Item: Is this company providing a win-win for its entire ecosystem?

Case Study Three: What Lies Beneath?

My study of companies like Wal-Mart and Costco led me to invest in CarMax—the Wal-Mart or Costco of secondhand cars. Since opening its first store in Virginia in 1993, CarMax has sold over 4 million cars, and it currently boasts about a hundred stores across America. It's a highly efficient operation with a narrow spread between what it pays for cars and the price at which it sells them. Customers know that the sales prices in its big-box stores are among the lowest around. And there's a huge selection of cars on display, ranging from two-year-old Mercedes SUVs to Mustang convertibles from the 1950s.

There is one other key aspect to the CarMax business model: it provides customers with access to financing. In the United States, a significant portion of cars are leased. Without financing, many CarMax customers wouldn't be able to buy its cars. In fact, if CarMax were to find that it couldn't access the debt markets, its whole business model would fall apart. And in 2008 it did fall apart. Sales plummeted because CarMax and its customers could no longer obtain credit amid the global financial crisis. As a result, the stock price crashed.

Once again, I discovered the importance of understanding a company's entire value chain. I hadn't given sufficient thought to just how dependent CarMax was on the credit markets, and how vulnerable this made the business. I might well have made the purchase anyway. After all, I could never have predicted the severity of the credit crisis. But this situation taught me how critical it is to discern whether a business is overly exposed to parts of the value chain that it can't control. If this is the case (as it often is), I need to be compensated for that heightened risk with a lower purchase price.

In response to this experience, I developed a checklist item that allows me to get a deeper sense of the quality of the business. One way to word this item might be: "Are the company's revenues leveraged to the credit markets?" But I don't get too hung up on the exact wording that I use in my checklist. A more general version of this item might be: "How does this company sit within the value chain, and what parts of this business could be impacted by changes in other parts of the value chain that this company has very little influence over?" The point is that I want to invest in companies that control their own destiny, not in companies that have their destiny determined by forces beyond their control.

It's also possible to use this way of thinking to identify some great investment opportunities. The goal in these situations is to find companies where one aspect of the value chain has gone awry, dragging down the whole business. If I believe this problem is temporary, I can buy the stock at a beaten-down price and then benefit once this issue within the value chain is resolved.

In 2007 this thought process led me to invest in Alaska Milk, the dominant producer of condensed milk in the Philippines. The company's key ingredient was powdered milk that had to be imported from abroad. When the global price of powdered milk shot up, the company's profit margins were squeezed and its stock plunged. I was convinced that the price of powdered milk would eventually return to normal as supply rose to match increased demand from China. As a result, Alaska Milk's profits would rebound. This proved correct, and I made about five times my money in five years.

Checklist Item: How could this business be affected by changes in other parts of the value chain that lie beyond the company's control? For example, are its revenues perilously dependent on the credit markets or the price of a particular commodity?

Case Study Four: How I Lost My Balance

Smart Balance, which has since been renamed Boulder Brands, was an innovative food company led by a superstar marketer named Stephen Hughes. Its flagship product is a blend of vegetable and fruit oils that competes with leading margarines such as Shedd's Country Crock and I Can't Believe It's Not Butter. Smart Balance's spread is based on an oil-blending process patented by food scientists at Brandeis University, and it offers a genuinely healthy alternative to rival spreads that are rich in trans-fatty acids. By contrast, Smart Balance's spread is said to lower consumers' "bad" cholesterol and to raise their "good" cholesterol. Following its launch in 1997, it breezed past Land O'Lakes to become the number-three brand in the margarine category.

As a longtime shareholder of Nestlé, I had seen "functional" products like this become a fast-growing and increasingly profitable niche within the food industry. I figured that Smart Balance, as a smaller and nimbler player, would grow rapidly for the next five or so years in both the margarine category and related businesses such as peanut butter and popcorn. At that point, it would get bought out by a larger competitor. I also liked the fact that Smart Balance had outsourced its manufacturing and distribution, so it was a pure marketing and branding company. And its management team was quite something.

Hughes enjoyed a remarkable reputation. He had famously turned around Tropicana's juice business in the United States before achieving similarly impressive feats with brands like Celestial Seasonings tea and Silk Soymilk. An article about Smart Balance in *Fortune* began with the line, "Success has followed Steve Hughes wherever he has roamed in the food industry over the past two decades." Hughes himself was quoted as saying, "We are positioning this as a brand that could grow to a billion dollars, a true mega-brand."

Back then, I hadn't yet abandoned my practice of meeting with management. Hughes came to my office, and I quickly fell under his spell. It wasn't just that he had a superb résumé. He was also incredibly smart and charismatic—a wonderful guy who, for good reason, was widely liked and admired. Already, his top-notch team had been successful in gaining distribution for Smart Balance at Wal-Mart, and I observed for myself how much shoppers there liked the brand. At the same time, an analyst who was working for me loved the stock and was desperate for me to buy it, partly because it was frustrating to work for a long-term investor who so rarely acquired a new holding. Confident that we had found a winner, I bought Smart Balance in 2007. There was just one problem. I overpaid.

Of course, I didn't realize this at the time. The stock had just fallen more than 30 percent from its peak. But it still traded at a high multiple of its current earnings and cash flow. I made the classic mistake of thinking about the valuation in relative terms. I should simply have asked myself, "Is it cheap in absolute terms?" Instead, I reassured myself that it was *relatively* cheap now that the price had dropped from its highs. I was also banking on Hughes to justify this steep valuation by delivering on his ambitious growth targets. Given his—and my—vision of a glorious future, I thought Smart Balance was a steal.

What followed was no catastrophe, but it was hardly the triumph I had expected. When the financial crisis struck, consumers reined in their spending on higher-priced items like Smart Balance margarine; instead of fretting about their bad cholesterol, they fretted about their finances. It didn't help that Smart Balance's rivals, stung by its success, retaliated with a price war that further eroded profits.

Hughes and his team responded well in a tough environment. They kept a careful watch on pricing. Seeing the importance of offering a cheaper product, they also acquired a value brand called Best Life. Throughout this difficult period, the company generated a lot of free cash, which it deployed intelligently for marketing, debt reduction, and share repurchases. It was hard to complain, given that they did everything right. Still, by the time I finally cashed out of the stock in 2012 after five long years, I had lost about 30 percent of my money.

I had only myself to blame. I had paid a high entry price that was justified only if the company lived up to its full potential. I made the mistake of basing my investment on what this superstar manager might achieve with his promising brand instead of focusing on the value of the business as it existed at the time of my purchase. Without Hughes at the helm, knowledgeable buyers from within the food industry would probably have acquired Smart Balance for 60 to 70 percent of the price that I had paid to invest. I should have paid even less. This would have saved me a lot of heartache. I had also overlooked the reality that all brands are not created equal: Smart Balance was a fine brand with plenty of upside, but it was no Nestlé.

I've bought many cheap stocks over the years, but I'm intermittently astounded by my capacity to pay an excessive price for what I perceive to be a high-quality business. This flaw lay at the heart of my mistake in buying Smart Balance. A key lesson for me is that, in the long run, I will save an awful lot of money if I succeed in countering this tendency to overpay. This should also save a lot of my brain cells. After all, if I pay too much up front, I'd better understand everything there is to know about the company since there is no margin of safety. If I invest when it's undervalued, I can be wrong about a whole host of issues and still make a good return.

This kind of self-awareness is vital since you can only design a checklist to address your weaknesses if you know what those weaknesses happen to be. To cite a similar example, I also overpaid for shares in Discover Financial Services (DFS), a credit card business that was spun out from Morgan Stanley in 2007. In retrospect, I can see that one idiosyncratic reason why I was drawn to DFS was that it was so intellectually difficult to analyze: it was a highly profitable company, but it's such a complex business that it was virtually impossible to know whether the moat around it would widen or narrow. My internal monologue went something like this: "All these other investors think this stock is too expensive. But they're just not smart enough to appreciate the subtleties that make this such an incredible purchase. I, on the other hand, am not fearful of paying a high price because I'm smarter and can understand the nuances that they're missing."

People like me—who pride ourselves on being clever and well educated—are particularly prone to this type of narcissistic hubris. We can easily get caught up in analyzing companies that, like DFS, should really be relegated to what Buffett calls the "too hard" pile. Unfortunately, I wasn't sufficiently aware of these dangerous tendencies of mine back then. So I bought DFS at around $26 per share in January 2006 despite its analytical complexities. I soon came to regret it.

At the height of the credit crisis, the stock fell below $5, and I couldn't be absolutely certain that the business would survive. I didn't want to compound my mistake of overpaying for it with the equally dumb mistake of selling it prematurely. So I held on. The stock rebounded sharply before I finally sold it in November 2011 for around $24—not far from my original purchase price. Still, I could have avoided all of this pain and frustration if I had been more keenly aware of those dual weaknesses of mine: my tendency to overpay and my irrational enthusiasm for analytical challenges that make me feel smart. These bruising experiences with Smart Balance and DFS led me to add some additional items to my checklist.

Checklist Items: Is this stock cheap enough (not just in relative terms)? Am I sure that I'm paying for the business as it is today—not for an excessively rosy expectation of where it might be in the future? Does this investment satisfy me psychologically by meeting some unmet personal need? For example, am I keen to buy it because it makes me feel smart?

12

DOING BUSINESS THE
BUFFETT-PABRAI WAY

SITTING ON MY SHELF IN ZURICH IS A BOOK CALLED
The 48 Laws of Power by Robert Greene. It has apparently sold more
than 1.2 million copies in the United States alone and has been hailed
by *Fast Company* as a "mega cult classic." You can get a flavor of its
dark message by pondering "Law 14," which recommends that we
should "Pose as a Friend, Work as a Spy." A brief summary of this law
explains: "Knowing about your rival is critical. Use spies to gather
valuable information that will keep you a step ahead. Better still: Play
the spy yourself. In polite social encounters, learn to probe. Ask indi-
rect questions to get people to reveal their weaknesses and intentions.
There is no occasion that is not an opportunity for artful spying."

In some ways, this scheming Machiavellian, approach to life and
business is quite seductive. In my youth, there was a part of me that
certainly identified with it, fancying myself as a budding Gordon
Gekko, with the intelligence and cunning to manipulate my way
to the top. And as my experience at D. H. Blair taught me, there is
plenty of opportunity on Wall Street for cynical operators to get rich
by putting their own interests first. But as I later discovered, there is
also a more enlightened path to success, even within the dog-eat-dog

financial world—an approach that I have come to think of as "The Buffett-Pabrai Way."

By observing Warren and Mohnish—both from a distance and up close—I gradually learned to become a better investor, a better businessman, and (I hope) a better person. This process began when I first read Lowenstein's biography of Buffett during my time at D. H. Blair. That book changed me because it filled my head with Buffett's thoughts, introducing me to the right person and the right ideas at a critical moment when I desperately needed guidance to get out of the moral maze in which I was lost. Indeed, the best way to learn is to surround yourself with the right people. As Warren told Mohnish and me at our charity lunch: "Hang out with people better than you, and you cannot help but improve."

Those words have had an enormous impact on me. As Buffett helped me to understand, nothing is more important than getting better people into your life. To put it another way, relationships are the killer app. Indeed, I'm convinced that this is the single most important way that we can tilt the playing field in our favor to achieve success as investors and in other areas of life. How, then, do we create and nurture the right relationships so that we can learn from them what we need to learn and become who we ought to be?

I'm not sure that I fully grasped the overwhelming importance of our peer group until I came across a fascinating book and a subsequent TED talk by Nicholas Christakis. He and his colleagues at Harvard had studied obesity in human networks, and this research led them to an important discovery: if you have obese friends, you're more likely to be obese. Similarly, if you have fit and healthy friends, you're more likely to be fit and healthy. In other words, our close social connections count not only in the obvious ways, but also in subtle ways that we barely understand.

I have no doubt that this is also the case in business. If so, it stands to reason that I should make a conscious effort to have the best possible people in my social networks. At first, I approached this idea in a calculated and self-serving manner, hoping that my attempts to build "social capital" would lead me to greater financial and professional success. But the relationships that I began to form were so life enriching that my cynical motives gradually receded. I'm not saying that I'm Mahatma Gandhi. But my deepening bonds with great people became a source of such sincere joy to me that I no longer needed any hidden agenda: these friendships became a wonderful end in themselves, not a means to self-advancement.

Serendipitously, I'm writing these words in the Delamar Greenwich Harbor Hotel in Connecticut—the very place where I had my first dinner with Mohnish a decade ago, on February 11, 2004. That meeting led to a friendship that has been one of the greatest pleasures of my life—a relationship that really illustrates everything that I hope to convey in this chapter.

Just yesterday, I received an email from Mohnish with the subject line: "Need to put book on hold. The next idea is Upon Us!!!!" His five-word email message then named an Asian company, along with the phrase "a 4x!" In other words, he'd found a stock that he thought could go up four-fold, and he wanted me to know about it too. At the same time, he trusted me to look into it further and give him a useful second opinion, just as Buffett has, for decades, turned to Charlie Munger—though, admittedly, the quality of the response might be a tad higher in Charlie's case.

Think about this. Here is Mohnish, one of the great investors of our time, happily sharing his latest investment idea with me. At one level, this act of kindness could be a tremendous financial gift for me and my shareholders if my research leads me to the same conclusion and I buy the stock. But at a deeper level, that simple email is a gift of true friendship—an act of sharing, trust, generosity, and affection. This act is also built on an understanding of the unsurpassed power of friendship—a recognition that, when we join together with good intentions, we are much more than the sum of our parts. As Mohnish often says, quoting an old adage that Ronald Reagan loved, "There's no limit to what you can do if you don't mind who gets the credit." What more could I ask for than a friend like this?

I hope that I'm making this sufficiently clear because it's almost certainly the most important point in this book—even though it may seem blindingly obvious to you. Nothing, nothing at all, matters as much as bringing the right people into your life. They will teach you everything you need to know.

In countless ways, this relationship with Mohnish has been an eye-opening education for me. For example, over the past ten years, I've repeatedly observed how he looks to see what he can do for others, not the other way around. He never sat me down and explained the thinking behind this behavior. I simply witnessed how he acted with me and with others, and I tried my best to learn from it. I saw how he would focus first on creating a real relationship and would then constantly look for ways to give, not take. He wasn't pushy. He didn't put people under any obligation. He seemed simply to ask himself, "What can I do for them?" Sometimes this was a kind word or a piece of advice; sometimes it was an introduction to someone else; sometimes it was a book that he would send as a gift and as a way of saying that he was thinking of that person.

By acting in this way, I could see that Mohnish created an incredible network of people who wish him well and would love to find ways to help him and thank him for his kindness. This is the extraordinarily powerful effect of compounding goodwill by being a giver, not a taker. And as he has taught me, the paradox is that you end up receiving infinitely more in life by giving than by taking. There's a real irony here: in focusing on helping others, you end up helping yourself too. For some people, this is not easy to understand. They act instead as if life were a zero sum game, in which the person who gives something away is the poorer for it.

Buffett, of course, understands this perfectly, thanks in no small part to the influence and example of his late wife, Susan, who was the kindest and most giving of people. After visiting her in hospital, he told a class at Georgia Tech, "When you get to my age, you'll really measure your success in life by how many of the people you want to have love you actually love you. I know people who have a lot of money, and they get testimonial dinners and they get hospital wings named after them. But the truth is that nobody in the world loves them. If you get to my age in life and nobody thinks well of you, I don't care how big your bank account is, your life is a disaster. That's the ultimate test of how you have lived your life."

He continued, "The trouble with love is that you can't buy it. You can buy sex. You can buy testimonial dinners. You can buy pamphlets that say how wonderful you are. But the only way to get love is to be lovable. It's very irritating if you have a lot of money. You'd like to think you could write a check: I'll buy a million dollars' worth of love. But it doesn't work that way. The more you give love away, the more you get." Of all the lessons that Warren has taught me, perhaps this is the most important.

Anybody who sees Buffett merely as a great stock picker is clearly missing the point. At our charity lunch, his kindness and generosity of spirit were unmistakable. He was evidently determined to deliver much more value to us than we could possibly have hoped for or expected. He was there to give, both to the GLIDE Foundation and to us, not to receive. He wasn't just polite and cordial. He was there with every ounce of his being, trying to make this an occasion that we would never forget. Here was one of the richest men in the world, a man who could gain nothing from us, yet he took the care to treat us this way.

I also saw this in the years that followed when he made the effort to give Mohnish and me a tour of his office or to send me a note that said something like, "Enjoyed reading your annual report, Guy." This message, scrawled in a few seconds, was a small act of kindness that—coming from him—meant the world to me. If there's a reward for acting this way, I would suggest that it's simply the happiness and lightness of heart that he derives from this approach to life. I don't

believe that he behaves this way with any agenda. But Warren, like
Mohnish, innately understands that this is the way the universe works:
the more we give, the more we receive. Warren's life is one of the great
examples of this benevolent cycle.

But perhaps the most important point to make here is that this is
how we learn—by watching people who are better than us, modeling
their behavior, then experiencing for ourselves why their approach
is wise and works. The point is not to lionize Warren or Mohnish,
who have flaws and foibles just like the rest of us. It's to share this idea
that there is no more important aspect of our education as investors,
businesspeople, and human beings than to find these exceptional role
models who can guide us on our own journey. Books are a priceless
source of wisdom. But people are the ultimate teachers, and there may
be lessons that we can only learn from observing them or being in
their presence. In many cases, these lessons are never communicated
verbally. Yet you feel the guiding spirit of that person when you're
with them.

One of my favorite examples of this is from Li Lu's introduction
to the Chinese edition of *Poor Charlie's Almanack*. He tells a wonderful anecdote about Charlie Munger in which, no matter how early he
showed up for an appointment, Munger was always there before him.
Each time, Li Lu would show up earlier and earlier. And each time,
Munger was already there. Eventually, Li Lu was showing up as much
as one hour early, so they would each read their newspapers separately
until the meeting began at the appointed time. Apparently, Charlie
had once been late for an important meeting through no fault of his
own, and he had vowed to himself never to let it happen again.

As for Warren, he's a social animal and has built an ecosystem
around himself of remarkable people who reflect and reinforce his
own values. His inner circle includes Charlie Munger, Bill Gates, Ajit
Jain, Debbie Bosanek, and Carol Loomis. But there are many others
too. These people look out for him, and he looks out for them. Again
and again, he has proved to be an astute judge of character, allying

himself with outstanding people and making amazingly few mistakes. At times, I suspect that he bought certain companies not just because these were great businesses, but because they were run by great people whom he wanted in this ecosystem—people like Thomas Murphy (who headed Capital Cities/ABC) and Rose Blumkin. He loved to tell stories about Blumkin's astonishing work ethic, and he clearly saw her as a role model.

In my own experience, there are countless ways of improving the circles in which we operate. Some of these are so obvious that it's tempting not to mention them at all. But these simple, practical steps have made such a difference to my life that I'll briskly mention some of them, even at the risk of sounding trite. For example, I joined various organizations where I could regularly rub shoulders with people who are better than me in a multitude of ways. This includes two extraordinary business groups that teach leadership qualities: the Entrepreneurs' Organization and the Young Presidents' Organization. I also joined Toastmasters, which teaches leadership through public speaking. Likewise, I met with a wonderful assortment of value investors once a month at Manhattan's Colbeh restaurant as part of a group organized by Shai Dardashti. Some of my most valuable business relationships grew out of these monthly lunches.

Having seen how much it helps to be part of a group like this, I later teamed up with John Mihaljevic to create VALUEx as a place where "like-minded people can develop their worldly wisdom, learn to be better investors, and become better people in the process." The goal is to build a community in which we can all have a positive influence on one another. After all, it's so much easier to stay on track when you have support instead of going it alone. For similar reasons, my family became members of the local Jewish community in Zurich. As Christakis had shown me, our peer group has a far-reaching influence on us. So I figured that being a member of a religious community would increase the odds that we would elevate ourselves spiritually and morally as a family—much as I figured that attending the annual meetings of Berkshire in Omaha and Wesco in Pasadena would elevate me as an investor.

Initially, I had thought that participating in groups and events like these would allow me to meet better people and that these contacts would help me to advance myself. Certainly, there are benefits to that kind of networking. But for me, the greatest benefit to hanging out in these positive environments was a more subtle one: the opportunity to observe people who were far better at business and life than I was. This is one of the many reasons why attending Berkshire's annual meeting is such a rich learning experience. For example, one year, I was having a drink in Omaha with a friend named Jonathan Brandt when I noticed that Don Keough was standing nearby. Keough is a renowned business leader who has served on the boards of companies like Berkshire, Coca-Cola, and McDonald's. He recognized Jonathan (whose father had been Buffett's stockbrocker), exchanged some thoughts with him, then took the trouble to introduce himself to me. I had an electric feeling, as if all his energies were focused on me. For that instant, I felt like I was the only person who mattered to him.

Of course you could say that this was simply the polite and decent behavior that we should expect from anyone, which is true. But even a fleeting encounter like this helped me to discern some of the qualities that allow people to shine in business. For example, I could see from Keough's impact on me just how important it is to be fully present and engaged whenever I meet someone—particularly if that person is at an earlier stage in their career, or if they might be ill at ease. His example made me aspire to be better so that my own meetings with strangers might one day be similarly memorable and genuine.

Likewise, I'm struck by how often and enthusiastically Buffett speaks to MBA students. It's a time in their lives when they are particularly open to new ideas. And if they haven't yet secured a post-MBA job, they might also feel a little vulnerable. So his generous spirit may mean all the more to them. There's a great lesson in this for me: if Warren can take the time to act like this with students (not to mention with investors like me), then I too need to act with real kindness toward the students I meet at business schools, and I should also respond encouragingly to every young graduate who sends me a résumé.

At our lunch, Mohnish asked Warren how he's managed to select the right people with whom to associate. Warren replied that he can survey a room filled with a hundred people and easily identify the ten he'd do business with and the ten he'd avoid. The other 80 would go into his "not sure" category. At the time, I didn't find this insight particularly satisfying. But I later realized that I should have applied this thinking before going to work for D. H. Blair. There had been enough smoke to raise real concerns about the existence of fire, including the critical article I had read about the firm in the *New York Times*. On that basis alone, the company and its charismatic leader Morty Davis should have gone into my own "not sure" category. Temperamentally, I like to be fair and to give people the benefit of the doubt. But in this instance, circumspection would have served me better. In any case, the key lesson from Warren was to invest time and energy in the handful of people you're sure about and leave the rest alone.

On this basis, I decided that I needed to become more efficient at eliminating people from my network if I wasn't sure about them. The first place where I applied this idea was in my hiring process. I had originally assumed that the right way to hire is to place an advertisement and then sift through the many résumés that came my way, trying to give every candidate the benefit of the doubt. After all, this is how consulting firms and investment banks did it when they went about hiring people like me. But one well-documented problem with this approach is that a high proportion of these job candidates have some attribute that makes them hard to employ while the best candidates get snapped up fast. Those who don't get snapped up fast also tend to get better at disguising their flaws, which become harder and harder to discern.

So I stopped advertising. Instead, I ended up hiring people whose behavior I had a chance to observe in unguarded moments. For example, I hired Dan Moore as an analyst after contacting him about a piece of equity research he had done. He wouldn't share it with me because I wasn't a client of his buy-side firm. The exemplary way that he handled this situation showed me the high quality of his ethics and his loyalty to his employer. This insight into his character was a key reason for my offering him a job. Likewise, I hired Orly Hindi, my director of operations, after meeting her at a Colbeh dinner, where I saw how gracefully she handled a difficult social encounter. This provided me with a perfect example of her remarkable people skills. Indeed, my most successful hires have happened not because I advertised the position, but because I observed the person in candid moments like these, when they were simply being themselves.

At the same time, I also consciously moved away from dealing with anyone who struck me as mysterious or opaque in any way. In my impressionable youth, I had a number of glittering, socially prominent "friends" who were obscure about who they really were. After leaving Oxford, I was naïvely dazzled by someone who claimed to be a Tatar prince. That summer, we gallivanted around London and the French Riviera, meeting other supposed princes and princesses. I found it exciting, and I enjoyed the feeling that I was entering these rarefied social circles. In a way, it was just a bit of frivolous fun, but it was also mildly pernicious to be captivated by this world of superficial glamour.

Mohnish showed me a better way. In his view, life is just too short to deal with people who aren't straightforward and forthcoming about who they are. The best strategy is simply to leave the mysterious obfuscators alone. The goal is not to figure them out, but to keep a distance. Warren and Mohnish, who are both down-to-earth and entirely lacking in pretense, are only interested in dealing with people who are an open book. They distance themselves from all the others, leaving them in the "not sure" category, which is the human equivalent of the "too hard" box on Warren's desk.

Before I have an appointment with a person I don't already know, I typically provide them with written information about myself—for example, my bio and my fund's annual report. I want to make it as easy as possible for them to see where I'm coming from and to form an accurate impression of me. Likewise, I routinely ask them to send me some background material about themselves. If people are enigmatic or elusive in any way, I apply Buffett's "not sure" rule and decide against a closer relationship.

By the same token, I hope they will see that I really am who I appear to be—not a fake who deceives either himself or others. I want to be the same person on the inside as on the outside. In business, as in other areas of life, I would argue that we attract people who are similar to us, who reflect the level of our own consciousness. If I strive to be honest and decent, I'm more likely to bring into my life people who are honest and decent. This helps to explain why Buffett has drawn such remarkable people into his orbit: they provide a reflection of who he is.

By observing Mohnish, I also learned another key lesson about how to behave, both in business and in other areas of life. I could see that he was never needy or demanding in the way that he dealt with people. There was no sense of entitlement or desire to encroach on their time. In the early days of our relationship, I'd call him in California and say apologetically, "I hope you're not busy and that I'm not disturbing you." He'd reply, "Busy? On the contrary, I was just twiddling my thumbs." It wasn't true, but it was his way of making me feel that nothing was more important than my call. Indeed, on countless occasions, I've received emails in which he says, "Call if you're twiddling." Similarly, when we traveled to Omaha to meet Debbie Bosanek for lunch in 2010, he wrote to her, "Our schedule is very flexible. . . . Feel free to suggest whatever is ideal for u."

This isn't a question of being sycophantic or losing his own sense of self. On the contrary, Mohnish has a healthy ego. But I've repeatedly seen how careful he is not to impose himself on others or to ride roughshod over their interests. He wants to show up only where he's needed or wanted. He takes great care not to be a burden to anyone or to make them feel that they have any obligation to him.

Watching him act like this had a profound impact on me because I could see so clearly that it was a great way to behave. I remember discussing with him a situation in which an investor wanted to sell his stake in my fund. My father initially suggested that I try to dissuade the person. But Mohnish told me, "Don't try to convince them. It's their money. If they want to take it out, let them do it, no questions asked." The relationship with my investor might have been ending, but Mohnish helped me to see that there should be no guilt or recrimination—and, above all, no sense of obligation.

This simple but robust idea has radiated out into many other areas of my life. To give you just one example, I never try to solicit my friends (or anyone else, for that matter) to invest in my fund. I'm happy for them just to be my friends. There is never any obligation.

Yet, looking back, I can see how appallingly needy I was in my early years as a fund manager. Back then, I had somehow convinced myself that it was important to sell myself and my fund to prospective investors, as if this brazen pushiness were an integral part of being a smart businessman and a high-flying fund manager. In reality, this was just an embarrassing example of my neediness. I also came to see what a turn-off it had been when I cold-called someone in an attempt to drum up business, or when I sent out a mass email in the vain hope of seizing the attention of prospective investors who had expressed no interest at all in the fund. This can only have made it *less* likely that discerning people would want to establish closer ties with me.

By contrast, I love the story of Ian Jacobs, a Columbia Business School graduate who successfully applied for a job with Buffett at Berkshire's headquarters. Along with his cover letter, Jacobs apparently enclosed a check to recompense Warren for his time in evaluating this job application. Some people saw this as a ridiculous gimmick. But the check—which I'm sure was never cashed—would have instantly communicated the message that Jacobs respected the value of Buffett's time. It was a powerful signal that he did not want to be a burden.

This is a smart way to act, not least because people get defensive when they sense that we want something from them or harbor a hidden agenda. I began to realize that my attempts to grab attention or impose myself on others were particularly annoying when I was dealing with important people since they are so often targeted in this way. Not long ago, I had an unforgettable lunch with the CEO of a major bank. Early in our meeting, I told him sincerely that I just felt so blessed in my life and so fortunate to be there with him. He relaxed visibly when he realized that I wasn't angling for anything but just wanted to enjoy his company. The key, in my experience, is to value people as an end in themselves, not as a means to our own ends.

Mohnish often quotes a beautiful line from the Bible, "I am but dust and ashes." Now, like me, he's a work in progress, and there's a hint of irony in his voice when he says this—as if to acknowledge that he has not quite reached this level of humility and self-abnegation. Neither of us could lay convincing claims to sainthood quite yet. Still, I've repeatedly seen his desire to serve others and not to put his needs above theirs. His example has helped me to understand that it's possible to be a servant without losing your autonomy, self-respect, or ambition. In my early years as a fund manager, I would have mocked the idea of being a servant. I preferred to see myself as a smart manipulator. But at our charity lunch Warren was also a servant of sorts despite being the world's most famous investor.

Thanks in large part to Mohnish and Warren, I began to realize that I ought to focus more on what others need from me instead of constantly trying to get them to fulfill my own needs. This might sound obvious, but it's been a huge psychological shift for me, and it's really changed the way that I live my life.

In my New York vortex days, I would go to a networking event, meet a stranger, and wonder how they could help me. Often, they'd talk *at* me about whatever product or service they wanted to sell, and I started to see how repulsive this sort of agenda-driven approach to business can be. So, over time, I developed a different attitude to networking. My simple rule was that, whenever I met someone, I would try to do something for them. It might simply be an introduction to someone else or even just a sincere compliment. What was intriguing to me was the way they reacted. In some cases, I sensed that they were saying to themselves, "That's nice. I wonder what else this guy is going to do for me, or what else I can ask him for." In other cases, I could see that they wanted to help me too. These seemingly trivial interactions provided a barometer of whether people approached the world as givers or takers.

At first, I attracted a high proportion of takers. For a while, I found myself getting ridiculously upset about it, wondering why they didn't understand that this was a lousy way to live. But by observing people closely, I gradually became a better judge of who was a giver and who was a taker, and I began to attract better people into my life. I hope this doesn't sound more calculated than it is. Because what I'm trying to do is simply create an ecosystem for myself in which everybody is the type of person who wants to find ways of helping others.

When you're surrounded by people like this, all of them trying to help one another, it sometimes feels like heaven on earth. People like Mohnish or John Mihaljevic, for example, are just gems—always looking to help, to support, to share. These are the keepers. The people we want in our inner circle. The people we should fly across the world to see if they live abroad. And, of course, this is what I need to be for others.

The crazy thing is that, when you start to live this way, everything becomes so much more joyful. There is a sense of flow and alignment with the universe that I never felt when everything was about what I could take for myself. Again, I don't want to make this sound like I'm some kind of saint. But this experience of finding ways to serve others has been so overwhelmingly positive that I now find myself looking for more and more opportunities to help. These days, my focus isn't just on helping individuals but also organizations, such as my Oxford college, Harvard Business School, and the Weizmann Institute. I recently realized that the Entrepreneurs' Organization doesn't have a chapter in Israel, so I set one up. I also learned that there was no TEDx event in Zurich, so I cofounded one.

I'm not telling you this to be self-congratulatory as there are countless people who do so much more good than I do. The point is simply that my life has improved immeasurably since I began to live this way. In truth, I've become increasingly addicted to the positive emotions awakened in me by these activities. I also love the deepening sense of connection that I've gained to so many great people and institutions. One thing is for sure: I receive way more by giving than I ever did by taking. So, paradoxically, my attempts at selflessness may actually be pretty selfish.

Warren and Mohnish, who are two of the smartest guys on earth, clearly understand this. As an investor and a businessman, Warren's achievements are almost inconceivable. Yet his greatest legacy may well be his philanthropic work in supporting the Bill and Melinda Gates Foundation, which could affect millions of people. Likewise, Mohnish hasn't devoted his considerable gifts to the single-minded pursuit of wealth. His Dakshana Foundation is already transforming the lives of countless young Indians, giving them opportunities that might otherwise be unthinkable. He has told me more than once that he would prefer to be remembered for Dakshana than as an investor.

The goal for the rest of us is not to be Warren Buffett or Mohnish Pabrai, but to learn from them. In big ways and small, I've come to see them both as grand masters in the game of life. To repeat that all-important line from Warren, "Hang out with people better than you, and you cannot help but improve."

13

THE QUEST FOR
TRUE VALUE

IF YOUR GOAL IN LIFE IS TO GET RICH, VALUE INVEST-
ing is pretty hard to beat. Sure, there are times when it falls out of
favor, when even the greatest practitioners find themselves dismissed
as fusty has-beens who have lost their touch. But it's such a robust and
fundamentally sound way to invest that it eventually regains its luster.
Irrational exuberance comes and goes. The quest for value endures.

Still, this is not just a stock-picking strategy that can make you
rich. To me, even the phrase itself—"value investing"—implies something deeper than merely accumulating the millions required to buy a
mansion in Greenwich, a ski chalet in Gstaad, and a gleaming Ferrari.
As Warren Buffett's life exemplifies, what we are also talking about
here is a quest for *true* value—for some kind of meaning that goes beyond money, professional advancement, or social cachet.

I don't mean to dismiss or deride those things. While I'm slightly
sheepish about my baser, more capitalist instincts, I'm not *that* sheepish . . . I do still drive a convertible Porsche, even though I'm mildly
embarrassed to admit it. And I'm so obsessed with my pursuit of the
perfect cappuccino that I spent $6,000 on an exquisite La Marzocco
coffee machine, which I imported from Florence. I try to justify these

excesses by contemplating the image of Sir John Templeton—who gave a fortune to charity—driving a Rolls Royce. Of course, even Buffett bought a private jet, which he self-mockingly named "The Indefensible." (Later, having changed his mind, he rechristened it "The Indispensable.") And, for that matter, Charlie Munger spent millions on a luxury catamaran called the "Channel Cat."

If stuff like this turns you on, then value investing is a great means to your self-indulgent ends. Enjoy. As I see it, this is the outer journey of the value investor—the quest for wealth, physical comfort, and (for want of a better word) success. But it's important not to get so caught up in this meaningless chase that we forget what matters most—the inner journey toward something less tangible yet more valuable. The inner journey is the path to becoming the best version of ourselves that we can be, and this strikes me as the only true path in life. It involves asking questions such as: What is my wealth for? What gives my life meaning? and how can I use my gifts to help others?

Relatively early in his investing career, Buffett closed down his limited partnerships and returned the assets to his shareholders. Even then, he just wasn't that interested in the unbridled pursuit of wealth. Clearly, it's not money that makes him tap dance to work. Likewise, Munger has said that, once you've made a certain amount (I think it was $100 million), there would have to be something wrong in your head for you to continue dedicating yourself to the accumulation of wealth. Templeton also devoted much of his life to the inner journey. Indeed, his greatest legacy is his charitable foundation, which explores "the Big Questions of human purpose and ultimate reality," including complexity, evolution, infinity, creativity, forgiveness, love, gratitude, and free will. The foundation's motto is "How little we know, how eager to learn."

In my experience, the inner journey is not only more fulfilling but is also a key to becoming a better investor. If I don't understand my inner landscape—including my fears, insecurities, desires, biases, and attitude to money—I'm likely to be mugged by reality. This happened early in my career, when my greed and arrogance led me to D. H. Blair. My desperate need to appear successful then made it difficult to admit my mistake and leave the company quickly after concluding that it was a morally corrosive environment. Later, in my New York vortex years, my envy of people with bigger funds and more glamorous homes led me astray again, convincing me that I needed to market myself and try to become something that wasn't true to who I am.

By embarking on the inner journey, I became more self-aware and began to see these flaws more clearly. I could work to overcome them only once I acknowledged them. But these traits were so deep-seated that I also had to find practical ways to navigate around them. For example, by moving to Zurich, I physically removed myself from an environment in Manhattan that exacerbated my greed and envy. Knowing that cities like New York and London—the epicenters of Extremistan—had this destabilizing effect on me, it seemed safest to get away.

But this is an ongoing process. As I write, my wife is exploring the possibility of moving our family to London so that we can be closer to my parents, my sister, and our children's cousins. In some ways, this scares me. Will I be able to deal with the emotional turmoil that London, with its extremes of wealth, might stir in me? Have I grown enough internally that I can move there without being emotionally destabilized? Can I create a peaceful environment for myself even within London—for example, in a quiet suburb, far from the reality distortion of the "super-prime" areas—where my mind can remain a calm pond? At the moment, the answers are unclear. But this is all part of my inner journey as I grapple with the idiosyncrasies that make it hard for me to be a rational investor.

Ignorance is not bliss when it comes to investing because the financial markets are mercilessly effective at exposing these emotional weaknesses. During the credit crisis, for example, it was vital to understand my own complex attitude to money since this affected my judgment and my ability to deal with the psychological impact of the crashing stock market. Intellectually, it's easy enough to master the technical tools of investing—the ability to read balance sheets, say, and to identify undervalued companies. But what good are these skills to investors who are drowning in a sea of fear that utterly overwhelms the rational neocortex?

Taking personal responsibility rather than blaming others is crucial. Instead of criticizing the fickle shareholders who bailed out of my fund at the bottom of the market, it was much more useful for me to think carefully about what it would mean to me if the market continued to crash and I had to close my fund. Why would it be so unbearably painful?

For me, this inner aspect of the market meltdown was very different than it was for Mohnish, who seemed entirely unaffected by the plunging prices of the stocks in his portfolio. As Mohnish tells it, he spent an important part of his youth witnessing the many ups and downs of his father's business career. Apparently, there were multiple occasions when his father was on the brink of financial collapse or actually went broke. Yet even amid that tumult, his family interactions were remarkably serene. So for Mohnish, the prospect of financial disaster is not as emotionally fraught as it might be for me. One happy result of his emotional fortitude was that he was able to keep buying busted stocks at a point when other investors might have been more inclined to curl up in a fetal position in a quiet corner of the office.

My own attitude to money is deeply influenced by the painful history of European Jewry. My great-grandparents were wealthy German industrialists who owned a major hat factory outside Berlin. Then the Nazis seized their assets and destroyed their life of privilege. My family escaped to Israel (then Palestine), where they set about reconstructing what they had lost. My grandfather, who had been a lawyer in Germany, became an unsuccessful Israeli chicken farmer. I grew up hearing tales of food shortages and of young men going off to defend the country during those early years in Israel. My father, having grown up on his parents' chicken farm, spent much of his career as a corporate salary man; he then started a business that generated excess cash, which I invested for him. By now, I've multiplied our family's wealth five-fold. But I still have a deep-seated fear that factors beyond my control could sweep everything away.

Why does any of this matter? Because this narrative subtly but powerfully shapes my entire approach to business and investing. For example, I never use borrowed money, and all my investments are sober and conservative. For me, the story of my family and money has been one of restoration—of fixing the damage that Hitler wrought. I feel a tremendous sense of responsibility when it comes to my family's finances (most of which are invested in my fund), not least because I'm attempting to repair what was shattered more than 70 years ago and to provide enduring security in an insecure world. I love what I do, but this is a serious business for me. And we know that money is closely associated with survival in the human mind, so these emotional issues have the potential to torpedo my rational brain. By contrast, Mohnish can buy stocks with a higher level of uncertainty and volatility since, for him, the possibility of loss doesn't trigger the kind of fears that are hardwired into my system.

I would argue that serious investors need to understand the complexities of their relationship to money, given its capacity to wreak havoc. Based on that understanding, we can make adjustments—for example, changing our physical environment or adding certain items to our investment checklist. But I'm not convinced that it's entirely possible to change the wiring itself, however smart we might be. I certainly haven't managed it yet. I used to think that I could overcome my fear of financial loss, thereby freeing myself to take more risk and achieve higher returns. But I've gradually come to accept that this is just part of who I am. There's no doubt that Warren and Mohnish have inner landscapes that better equip them to make clearheaded decisions involving money. But I can't spend my life yearning to be them. Instead, I need to understand what makes me different, then make investments that I can handle emotionally, based on this self-knowledge.

In the end, I handled the financial crisis well, partly because I confronted my fears of loss and found ways to work around them. If I hadn't been aware of this aspect of my inner life, I might have panicked when a stock like Discover Financial Services fell 80 percent. Instead, I held steady as it rebounded. Having gained a deeper sense of who I am, I've also stopped worrying about trying to get the best returns. I'm more comfortable aiming for decent returns that beat the market indexes over the long term despite my personal limitations. Similarly, I've always invested a hefty portion of my fund in Berkshire Hathaway. Given the company's enormous size, I could probably get better returns by investing elsewhere. But Berkshire's presence in my portfolio provides a ballast—both financially and emotionally. It's psychologically important to have Buffett in my ecosystem. Is this rational? For me, yes. For Mohnish, maybe not.

Given the importance of this inner journey, how—in practical terms—should we go about it? Personally, I've used countless tools to accelerate this process of inward growth, and I've found them all helpful (or interesting) at different stages of my life. I've done lots of psychotherapy, even though this would have appalled me in my closed-minded youth. Among other things, I did seven years of Jungian therapy once a week, and I've dabbled in things like emotionally focused therapy, cognitive behavioral therapy, neurolinguistic programming, and even eye movement desensitization and reprocessing. As I came to realize, humans are infinite in their variety, and there is an almost infinite variety of therapies to help us undertake this journey.

I've also delved into religion with various rabbis and other spiritual teachers, including my friend Isaac Sassoon, who is the author of a book called *Destination Torah: Reflections on the Weekly Torah Readings*. I've had regular sessions with career coaches. I've studied philosophy and became friends with Lou Marinoff, a "philosophical counselor" who is the author of *Plato, Not Prozac! Applying Eternal Wisdom to Everyday Problems*. And I've read countless self-help books. Temperamentally,

I'm not well suited to meditation. But I'm open to pretty much anything as long as I might learn something.

Another fantastic tool for internal growth is the experience of adversity. Indeed, this should really be the first tool of all. If we take responsibility for our mistakes and failures, they offer priceless opportunities to learn about ourselves and how we need to improve. My mistake in joining D. H. Blair, for example, enabled me to see that I had to deal with my avarice and also stop measuring myself by an outer scorecard. Adversity may, in fact, be the best teacher of all. The only trouble is that it takes a long time to live through our mistakes and then learn from them, and it's a painful process.

For me, the greatest springboard for the inner journey has been to participate in what Napoleon Hill would call a "mastermind" group. Harvard Business School calls it a study group, and the Young Presidents' Organization calls it "Forum." The name doesn't matter. The idea is for a close-knit group of about eight to ten professionals to share their issues confidentially, guided by a peer moderator. On one memorable occasion, I gave a 20-minute presentation about my tortured relationship with a key business associate who was also a close friend from university. The group then subjected me to two rounds of clarifying questions, which left all the details of the relationship out in the open for them to examine. My chest burned with anger. I was convinced that my friend had done things that were wrong and unfair and that she was taking advantage of me. But I also felt guilty and embarrassed since it became increasingly clear during this session that I hadn't behaved that well either.

Then, one by one, the other eight members of the group shared their own experiences of business relationships with friends or relatives that had gone awry. My first reaction was intense relief as I realized that I wasn't alone in making such mistakes. I also came to see that neither my friend nor I had acted quite as badly as I had believed. Equally important, nobody passed judgment on me, and I received no explicit advice since this would have violated the group's rules. Still, by the end of the discussion, I no longer felt that my guilt and anger were controlling me. And the eight stories were replete with examples of the type of actions that I could take to fix the situation. Instead of feeling powerless, I now had lots of options. As a result, I resolved my conflict in a positive way, and my former business associate remains a dear friend—and a shareholder in my fund—to this day.

Such is the power of a mastermind group—whether it's arranged by the Young Presidents' Organization, the Entrepreneurs' Organization, or a handful of trusted friends like the members of the Latticework Club, which Mohnish and I created. Twice a year, this group of eight professionals heads off for a three-day retreat to discuss whatever is on our minds. For me, meetings like these have been the single best accelerator of inner growth.

The truth is that it doesn't matter *how* you do this inner journey. What matters is that you do it. Whichever route you choose, the goal is to become more self-aware, strip away your façades, and listen to the interior. For an investor, the benefits are immeasurable because this self-knowledge helps us to become stronger internally and to be better equipped to deal with adversity when it inevitably comes. The stock market has an uncanny way of finding us out, of exposing weaknesses as diverse as arrogance, jealousy, fear, anger, self-doubt, greed, dishonesty, and the need for social approval. To achieve sustainable success, we need to confront our vulnerabilities, whatever they may be. Otherwise, we are building our success on a fragile structure that is ultimately liable to fall down.

But the real reward of this inner transformation is not just enduring investment success. It's the gift of becoming the best person we can be. That, surely, is the ultimate prize.

ACKNOWLEDGMENTS

WHEN SOMEONE HAS BEEN EXTRAORDINARILY GENEROUS, PER-
haps the best way to thank them is in writing—either in a letter to them or in a story
that attempts to recount their kindness. In that sense, this book is one long thank
you note to four of the greatest teachers in my life: my father, Simon Spier; Warren
Buffett; Charlie Munger; and Mohnish Pabrai. For me, the four of you are not just
a limitless well of wisdom but also an inspiring example of how to act in the world.

I also want to thank a number of people who made it possible for this book to
exist:

WILLIAM GREEN

What I thought would be light edits to the final draft quickly turned into a major
collaboration entailing heavy revision and entire rewrites of every chapter in record
time. Your compulsive dedication to making the text the very best that it can be, no
matter what the cost, has improved the book beyond my wildest expectations.

My own writing tends to come out in eddies, not to mention the occasional
wild vortex. You, on the other hand, know how to put sentences and paragraphs
together beautifully and in such a way that makes them a joy to read. Your sense of
narrative structure has shaped each and every chapter, ensuring that they had a beginning, middle, and end, not to mention a payoff for the reader.

More important, perhaps, through your rich knowledge of the subject matter
of the book, as well as of me, you were able to question me deeply. To push me to
complete half-finished thoughts and help me to surface ideas that I could not quite
figure out how to express. Even more impressive has been your regular capacity to
sense intuitively what I was reaching for and also put that into words.

This experience gave me the privilege of being able to learn more about writing from a master of the craft, and it leaves me with a newfound understanding and
respect for what great writers and editors do. I am deeply grateful to you for having
directed your talents toward me and this book for several intense months in Zurich,
Klosters, Greenwich, Shavei Tzion, and New York.

But perhaps the greatest reward of this collaboration has been the deeper friendship with you. To discover and enjoy your wicked sense of humor (including your
gleeful derision when I repeatedly spelled the word "the" as "teh"!), and by way of
your introduction to the Kabbalah, to discover new gates though which to connect
with the universal wisdom of the cosmos.

Thanks also to your wife, Lauren. And to your children, Henry and Madeleine:
I'm grateful to you for sharing your father's time with me. It was your temporary loss,
but a permanent gain for me and the reader.

JESSA GAMBLE

Without you, I never would have started this book because my fears of writing were simply too great. Upon first meeting you at TEDGlobal, I could see that you believed in my message and in this book even before I did. You alone sustained the idea of this book through our early conversations and interviews. You won the precious attention of William Clark, our agent. And, while I was quivering with fear, it was your excellent book proposal that brought us into the hands of Palgrave Macmillan and Laurie Harting.

Even once we started, there were many more moments than I care to remember when, had it not been for your constant and quiet encouragement, I might not have stuck with it. And your calming presence at our early morning writing sessions was instrumental in giving me the courage to face up to my terror and put pen to paper. But more than anything, thanks for your friendship and loyalty to me and to the book through the various changes and transformations of the project.

Thanks also to your son, Oliver, for having parted with you during your visits to Zurich.

LAURIE HARTING

At first, I think I was afraid of you! I had no idea why on earth you had taken such a risk with me. Let's not mince words: at the start, my writing was a bit of a mess. It is only as I gradually improved and began to understand what we were trying to create that I fully understood what a great ally, champion, and friend I had found in you. I can now see just how masterfully you have been able to coax the best out of me.

JENA PINCOTT AND PETER HORNICK

Thank you for your friendship and care, and for planting the first seeds of this book. Initially, those seeds fell on barren ground, but they did eventually find moisture and begin to germinate. You were always there through the dry spells to help and encourage me. And without you, the book would never have found its title.

COLLEAGUES

I had to fit the writing of this book in with my work as the manager of the Aquamarine Fund. Keith Smith, Lynda Brandt, and Orly Hindi: thank you so much for helping me to find the time and creating the structure for me to write. In this and so many other ways, you keep my life on track.

I am also grateful to the alumni of Aquamarine: Mariya Sklyar, Dan Moore, Jennifer Davies, Amanda Pullinger, David Kessler, Ori Eyal, Julie Schottenstein, Sahil Gujral, Mark Soukup, Pushkar Bedekar, Abhishek Rai, Sarah Stephenson, Oliver Suess, Meng Tian, and Rina Endo.

PRODUCTION

As this book has grown, it has attracted a growing band of incredible talent to produce it. In addition to the people mentioned above, many thanks to William Clark, my superb agent. Also, my thanks to Michelle Fitzgerald, Lauren LoPinto, Heather Florence, Alan Bradshaw, and the rest of the team at Palgrave Macmillan. Without your input and enthusiasm this book might simply have been a proposal, languishing in a drawer or filing cabinet. Thanks also to Mark Fortier for putting us on the map, to Charlie Campbell of the Ed Victor Literary Agency, to Cecelia Wong for your wonderful design of the book cover, and to Jelisa Castrodale for your care in fact-checking the manuscript.

PUBLISHING

Thanks also to Debbie Englander, Jenny and Jane-Anne Hobbs, Myles Thompson, Maggie Stuckey, and other friends from the publishing world who have helped in various ways to nudge this book along.

WRITING SPOTS

Early on, Lory (my wife) and I realized that I just had to write wherever I found myself, and so there are numerous places where this book was written. Eberhard von Koerber and Iris Schedler: our office in Zurich is truly an oasis. Joyce and Rene: so is Villa Florence, which you keep so immaculately. Flor Soriano, thanks for taking care of me and my family in Zurich and Klosters, and for helping to make our home such a warm environment. Thanks also to the kind and friendly staff at a whole host of other locations, including Via Quadronno, Ristorante Sant Ambroeus, Stumptown Coffee Roasters, Tmol Shilshom, Intelligentsia, Rizzoli, La Stanza, the New York Society Library, the London Library, the Zurich Central Library, Brasenose College, Uniklinik Balgrist, Widener Library, the Delamar Greenwich Harbor Hotel, Hotel Pardenn Piz Buin, Schulthess Klinik, Chesa Grischuna, the Mamilla Hotel, the Westin Resort Costa Navarino, Fess Parker Wine Country Inn & Spa, the Grasshopper Club, Hotel Irvine, Bacara Resort & Spa, the Racquet and Tennis Club of New York, La Palestra, the Phillips Club, the Queen's Club, the Tuxedo Club, and Paragraph.

TEACHERS

While helping me to write this book, William Green taught me a beautiful line from Henry James that life is "all inclusion and confusion" while art is "all selection and discrimination." In telling the story of my education as a value investor, there has—inevitably—been a great deal of selection since we couldn't include everything. This has meant that I haven't recounted in sufficient depth the importance of many great teachers in my life. Here, I want to thank these people who have been instrumental in my education:

I have been blessed with many extraordinary teachers and educators, including Peter Sinclair, Vernon Bogdanor, and Tony Courakis, who tutored me in economics and politics; Mary Stokes, John Davies, Hugh Collins, Peter Birks, and Bernard Rudden, who tutored me in law; and Diana Hughes, Charles Stewart, and others who taught me at the City of London Freemen's School. Richard Nolan, Dick Poorvu, Rawi Abdelal, Clayton Christensen, Boris Groysberg, Len Schlesinger, Jan Hammond, David Joffe, Amar Bhide, Bill Sahlman, and Ray Goldberg are some, but not all, of the brilliant professors I had at Harvard Business School.

In my professional life, I have also been tremendously fortunate to have had wonderful teachers and collaborators. John Mihaljevic: I am so grateful that you chose to move to Zurich when you did; I relish your friendship and our squash sessions! Ken Shubin Stein: our many conversations have served to deepen vastly my understanding of investing and how to implement the Buffett-Pabrai way in our own lives. Bryan Lawrence, Richard Bergin, Jane Buchan and Martin Calderbank: you showed me that business school does not have to be a shallow experience. Nick Sleep and Qais Zakaria: you have instructed me with great generosity, even if I have proved to be a poor student. Other colleagues, teachers, and friends from whom I have learned a great deal include Jonathan Brandt, Ciccio Azzolini, Gary Alexander, David Cameron, Chris Hohn, Lloyd Khaner, Girish Bhakoo, Allen Benello, Josh Tarasoff, Carley Cunniff, Shai Dardashti, Jeffrey Hamm, Bill Ackman, Boris Zhilin, Tom Gayner, Andy Kilpatrick, Amitabh Singhi, Franz Heinsen, Steve Wallman, Alice Schroeder, Eitan Wertheimer, Rolando Matalon, Tom Russo, Jens Heinemann, Vitaliy Katsenelson, Terry and Anne Plochman, Joanna Samuels, Norman Rentrop, Whitney Tilson, Rachel Gartner, Jack Skeen, Bruce Halev, Daniel Aegerter, Benjy Schmelz, Isaac Sassoon, Akshay Jain, Pasquale Manocchia, Diana Wais, Greg Peters, Peter Bevelin, Miguel Barbosa, Yaqub Hanna, Megh Manseta, Jeff Grant, Soren Ekstrom, Mo Fathelbab, Roni Witkin, Ken Tyler, Sanjeev Parsad, Gillian Ward, Michael Sanson, Debbie Bosanek, Satyabrata Dam, Ned Hallowell, Claude Chemtob, Michael Silverman, Jacob Wolinsky, Verne Harnish, Jono Rubinstein, Jorge Cherbosque, Ajay Desai, Susan Tross, Natasha Prenn, Mary Solanto, and Alex Rubalcava.

THE TED CONFERENCE

Thanks to Bruno Giussani at the TEDGlobal conference in Edinburgh, through whom I met Jessa Gamble, without whom this book would not have happened. I attended my first TED conference in Mysore, India, five years ago. At that conference, Chris Anderson's vision of "Ideas Worth Spreading" immediately took root in me, and I have been a regular attendee and participant in the community ever since. The TED conferences have contributed hugely to my becoming a more open, playful, and (hopefully) more enlightened person. Many thanks to everyone from TED who has touched my life, including Chris Anderson, Li Lu, Hugo Schotman, June Cohen, Jason Wishnow, Tom Wujec, Erik Brenninkmeijer, Lisa Stringle, Jane Wulf, Maya Elhalal-Levavi, Janet Echelman, Kathryn Schulz, Abigail Tenembaum, Claudia Marcelloni, Robert Gupta, Katherine McCartney, Lior Zoref, Michael Weitz, and Alex Knight. It was also through TED that I connected to my friend Rolf Dobelli of Zurich Minds, which has become another extraordinary force for change in my life.

PARTNERS, FRIENDS, AND FORUM MATES

I have been privileged to have a wonderful group of friends and forum mates who have taught me countless lessons about investing, business, and life. They include Tim Monahan, Jesper Hart-Hansen, John Meckert, Etienne Zackenfels, David Eigen, Stefan Rosen, Drew Pizzo, Len Katz, Marek Lis, Jim Tormey, Tony Coretto, Bryan David, Jay Lee, Ray Carile, Marc Stöckli, Vito Critti, Adrian Locher, Palo Stacho, Mark O'Malley, Christian Wey, Philip Ryffel, Jochen Werz, Nicolas Plakopitas, Jennifer Voss, Francisco Negrin, Jeremy Lack, Matt Weiss, Andrew Weeks, Spencer Young, Gilles Bonaert, Sarah Marshall, Roy Engel, Andreas Schweitzer, Daniel Schwartz, Grant Schreiber, Phong Nguyen, Beyla Ziv Guest, Chris Detweiler, Michael Baer, Mark Pincus, Maurice Ostro, Hossein Amini, Roger Glickman, Franz Heinsen, Kate Southgate, Jochen Wermuth, Harold Tittman, Perry Britton, Muna AbuSulayman, Naif al-Mutawa, Zohar Menshes, Patrick Questembert, Tim Beardson, Arturo Zapata, François Gutzwiller, Richard Harris, Arthur Mikaelyan, Anders Hvide, Fred Uytengsu, William O'Chee, Shira Kaplan, Karan Bilimoria, Luke Benfield, Charles Hipps, Bob Lowery, Frank Richter, Dana Hamilton,

Raffaello d'Andrea, Noemie Delfassy, Anil Kumar, Gene Browne, Yildiz Blackstone, Ahal Besorai, Andy Bender, David Rettig, Armin Struckmeier, David Somen, Andrew Weeks, Shimon Elkabetz, Adam Eiseman, Arthur Fish, Charles Dauber, Franziska Müller-Tiberini, Glenn Tongue, Adrian Beer, Shai Misan, Dominic Barton, Andy Bender, Lou Marinoff, Martin Seager, Phil Holthouse, Nick Soulsby, Eveline Carn, Sean Gorvy, Sarah Money, John Schwartz, Eyal Ronen, Philip and Herbert Ochtman, Jim Hawkins, Muhammad Habib, Peter Wilson, Sherry Coutu, Andrew Feldman, Stephanie Goff, Alan Hassenfeld, Sony Mordechai, Christian Stolz, Christina Anagnostara, Dan Sachs, Jeffrey Hamm, Stephen Roseman, Chung Mong-gyu, James Kralik, Yong Ping Duan, Ion Yadigaroglu, Jeff Pintar, and Dante Albertini. Organizations, forums, and other mastermind groups that have had a deep influence on me include various chapters of the Young Presidents' Organization and the Entrepreneurs' Organization, the Zuriberg and New York Pacers Toastmasters chapters, as well as the Posse, Fulani, Ararat, the Fawkes forum, the Latticework Club, and VALUEx.

MY EXTENDED FAMILY

Having lived in many countries, my deepest roots lie with my extensive family, scattered around the world from Mexico and the United States in the West to Israel and Australia in the East and to London, Munich, and Zurich in the middle. Saskia, Petra, Josh, Ramon, Gloria, Jules, Judy, Yochanan, Varda, Miriam, Amos, Ido, Zohar, Boaz, Michael, Shai, Hagai, Ori, Bridgit, Harvey, Jo, Clea, Hubertus, Raphael, Rosemarie, Klaus, Peter, Gaby, George, Frank, Rita, Dorothy, Selmar, Marlene, Paul, Erika, Andrea, Raquel, and all my other cousins: you have blessed me and my family with your rich diversity.

MY IMMEDIATE FAMILY

My father, Simon, who trusted me. My mother, Marilyn, who taught me empathy. My sister, Tanya: early on, I was able to learn vicariously from your experience. And that made my life immeasurably easier and my challenges so much more manageable.

My children: Sarah, Isaac, and Eva. Becoming a father has been an education in its own right, and I'm constantly astonished at how much you already know and have been able to teach me. It's been such a joy to see your growing knowledge and love of diverse subjects—from the Greek myths to *Star Wars,* from Harry Potter to the Berenstain Bears—and your burgeoning talents in sports and music. It's a marvel to see the way you move effortlessly between Spanish, English, German, and French, not to mention Hebrew. But each of you has also taught me in a deeper way: from you, I have learned more about qualities like empathy, playfulness, perseverance, and drive than I have learned from many adults. Thank you for being my ultimate teachers.

Finally, to my wife, Lory: thank you from the depths of my heart for giving me all of the time, love, and emotional support that I needed to write this book—and for putting up with me, my moods, and my distractions. With much gratitude and love,

Guy Spier
Zurich, 2014

BIBLIOGRAPHY AND GUIDE TO FURTHER READING

ALL OF THE BOOKS LISTED BELOW HAVE PLAYED A BIG PART IN MY education, not just as a value investor but as a person in search of happiness, fulfillment, and a deeper understanding of how the world works. My goal here is simply to share with you a selection of books that have had an impact on me and that have enriched my life. This is a decidedly idiosyncratic list, ranging from seminal works on investing to esoteric studies of complexity, psychology, and games. It's not a comprehensive list by any means. But I hope you'll find much in here that's useful, enlightening, and life-enhancing.

INVESTING

The Intelligent Investor: The Definitive Book on Value Investing by Benjamin Graham is where it all started for me. Four other books that deserve to be read and reread many times are Seth Klarman's *Margin of Safety: Risk-Averse Value Investing Strategies for the Thoughtful Investor;* Joel Greenblatt's *You Can be a Stock Market Genius: Uncover the Secret Hiding Places of Stock Market Profits; The Aggressive Conservative Investor* by Martin J. Whitman, Martin Shubik, and Gene Isenberg; and John Mihaljevic's *The Manual of Ideas: The Proven Framework for Finding the Best Value Investments.* Before I discovered value investing, I was also captivated by two other investment classics: Edwin Lefèvre's *Reminiscences of a Stock Operator* and *The Alchemy of Finance* by George Soros.

HEROES, MENTORS, AND ROLE MODELS

Roger Lowenstein's biography *Buffett: The Making of an American Capitalist* was the first book that I consciously used to help me "model" Warren Buffett. Other seminal works on Buffett include Alice Schroeder's *The Snowball: Warren Buffett and the Business of Life* and *Tap Dancing to Work: Warren Buffett on Practically Everything, 1966–2013* by his friend Carol Loomis, a renowned writer who worked at *Fortune* for 60 years. There is also a deep well of wisdom from Buffett in *Berkshire Hathaway Letters to Shareholders, 1965–2013.* Another marvelous glimpse inside the mind of a master is *Poor Charlie's Almanack: The Wit and Wisdom of Charles T. Munger,* which includes his eye-opening analysis of the causes of human misjudgment.

INNER EXPLORATIONS

The best guide to "forum" is Mo Fathelbab's *Forum: The Secret Advantage of Professional Leaders*. The title says it all. But I highly recommend that you discover the power of such mastermind groups by joining one. Some of the best are run by the Entrepreneurs' Organization and the Young Presidents' Organization, which devote enormous resources to helping their members have a positive forum experience. Toastmasters works slightly differently but is also excellent. (It's also a lot more egalitarian and a lot less expensive.) Alcoholics Anonymous, which I have not attended, produces a wonderful book entitled *Twelve Steps and Twelve Traditions*. Although created to help recovering alcoholics, its lessons are applicable to everyone.

SELF-HELP

It's tempting for cerebral people to raise their eyebrows at the very thought of self-help books, but I've found a great deal of practical wisdom within this genre. For me, the central figure here is Tony Robbins. *Awaken the Giant Within: How to Take Immediate Control of Your Mental, Emotional, Physical, and Financial Destiny!* provides as good an introduction as any to his ideas, as do his various recordings. But to experience the full benefit of what he has to teach, I would recommend attending one of his seminars.

PSYCHOLOGY

We all embark on the inner journey without a good road map. But there are signposts. I first began to discover this rich territory when I read *The Grail Legend* by Emma Jung and Marie-Louise von Franz, followed by *The Fisher King and the Handless Maiden: Understanding the Wounded Feeling Function in Masculine and Feminine Psychology* by Robert Johnson. During my seven-year stint in Jungian therapy, I found Edward Whitmont's *The Symbolic Quest: Basic Concepts of Analytical Psychology* a very useful handbook. My first explorations into the power of emotion came from reading Diana Fosha's *The Transforming Power of Affect: A Model for Accelerated Change*, which then led me to works by Allan Schore, Antonio Damasio, Joseph LeDoux, and others, some of which I've listed below.

A RANDOM WALK THROUGH MY LIBRARY

What follows is a brief list of additional books that I've found intriguing and enriching for countless reasons. Are they relevant to your education as an investor? Some yes. Some not so much. But I've found all of these books richly rewarding. They are filled with wisdom not just on stock-picking but on everything from ants to anarchy, finance to love. There should be something here for everyone.

Business

Delivering Happiness: A Path to Profits, Passion, and Purpose by Tony Hsieh
Different: Escaping the Competitive Herd by Youngme Moon
Getting to Yes: Negotiating Agreement without Giving In by Roger Fisher, William Ury, and Bruce Patton
Give and Take: Why Helping Others Drives Our Success by Adam Grant

How I Raised Myself from Failure to Success in Selling by Frank Bettger

Love Is the Killer App: How to Win Business and Influence Friends by Tim Sanders

Mastering the Rockefeller Habits: What You Must Do to Increase the Value of Your Growing Firm by Verne Harnish

Matsushita Leadership: Lessons from the 20th Century's Most Remarkable Entrepreneur by John Kotter

Ogilvy on Advertising by David Ogilvy

Overhaul: An Insider's Account of the Obama Administration's Emergency Rescue of the Auto Industry by Steven Rattner

Sam Walton: Made in America by Sam Walton with John Huey

The Box: How the Shipping Container Made the World Smaller and the World Economy Bigger by Marc Levinson

The Essays of Warren Buffett: Lessons for Corporate America by Warren Buffett and Lawrence Cunningham

The Go-Giver: A Little Story about a Powerful Business Idea by Bob Burg and John David Mann

The Halo Effect and the Eight Other Business Delusions That Deceive Managers by Phil Rosenzweig

The One Minute Manager by Kenneth Blanchard and Spencer Johnson

The Origin and Evolution of New Businesses by Amar Bhidé

The Power of Full Engagement: Managing Energy, Not Time, Is the Key to High Performance and Personal Renewal by Jim Loehr and Tony Schwartz

The Power of Habit: Why We Do What We Do in Life and Business by Charles Duhigg

The Startup Game: Inside the Partnership between Venture Capitalists and Entrepreneurs by William Draper

The Talent Code: Greatness Isn't Born: It's Grown, Here's How. by Daniel Coyle

Whale Done! The Power of Positive Relationships by Kenneth Blanchard, Thad Lacinak, Chuck Tompkins, and Jim Ballard

Who Moved My Cheese? An Amazing Way to Deal with Change in Your Work and in Your Life by Spencer Johnson

Working Together: Why Great Partnerships Succeed by Michael Eisner with Aaron Cohen

Economics

Modern International Economics by Shelagh Heffernan and Peter Sinclair

Predictably Irrational: The Hidden Forces That Shape Our Decisions by Dan Ariely

The Economy as an Evolving Complex System by Philip Anderson, Kenneth Arrow, and David Pines

The Rational Optimist: How Prosperity Evolves by Matt Ridley

Games

500 Master Games of Chess by S. Tartakower and J. du Mont

Homo Ludens: A Study of the Play Element in Culture by Johan Huizinga

Reality Is Broken: Why Games Make Us Better and How They Can Change the World by Jane McGonigal

Winning Chess Tactics for Juniors by Lou Hays

Wise Choices: Decisions, Games, and Negotiations by Richard Zeckhauser, Ralph Keeney, and James Sebenius

Investing

A Zebra in Lion Country by Ralph Wanger with Everett Mattlin

Active Value Investing: Making Money in Range-Bound Markets by Vitaliy Katsenelson

Beating the Street by Peter Lynch

Common Stocks and Uncommon Profits by Philip Fisher

Fooled by Randomness: The Hidden Role of Chance in Life and in the Markets by Nassim Nicholas Taleb

Fooling Some of the People All of the Time: A Long Short Story by David Einhorn and Joel Greenblatt

Fortune's Formula: The Untold Story of the Scientific Betting System that Beat the Casinos and Wall Street by William Poundstone

Investing: The Last Liberal Art by Robert Hagstrom

Investment Biker: Around the World with Jim Rogers by Jim Rogers

More Mortgage Meltdown: 6 Ways to Profit in These Bad Times by Whitney Tilson and Glenn Tongue

More Than You Know: Finding Financial Wisdom in Unconventional Places by Michael Mauboussin

Of Permanent Value: The Story of Warren Buffett by Andrew Kilpatrick

Pioneering Portfolio Management: An Unconventional Approach to Institutional Investment by David Swensen

Security Analysis by Benjamin Graham and David Dodd

Seeking Wisdom: From Darwin to Munger by Peter Bevelin

Short Stories from the Stock Market: Uncovering Common Themes behind Falling Stocks to Find Uncommon Ideas by Amit Kumar

The Dhandho Investor: The Low-Risk Value Method to High Returns by Mohnish Pabrai

The Manual of Ideas: The Proven Framework for Finding the Best Value Investments by John Mihaljevic

The Misbehavior of Markets: A Fractal View of Financial Turbulence by Benoit Mandelbrot and Richard Hudson

The Most Important Thing: Uncommon Sense for the Thoughtful Investor by Howard Marks

The Warren Buffett Way by Robert Hagstrom

Value Investing: From Graham to Buffett and Beyond by Bruce Greenwald, Judd Kahn, Paul Sonkin, and Michael van Biema

Where Are the Customers' Yachts? Or, A Good Hard Look at Wall Street by Fred Schwed

Your Money and Your Brain: How the New Science of Neuroeconomics Can Help Make You Rich by Jason Zweig

Literature

100 Years of Solitude by Gabriel García Márquez

Hamlet by William Shakespeare

Jonathan Livingston Seagull by Richard Bach

Oliver Twist by Charles Dickens

Zen and the Art of Motorcycle Maintenance: An Inquiry into Values by Robert Pirsig

Miscellaneous

Autobiography: The Story of My Experiments with the Truth by Mahatma Gandhi

City Police by Jonathan Rubinstein

Endurance: Shackleton's Incredible Voyage by Alfred Lansing

Long Walk to Freedom: The Autobiography of Nelson Mandela by Nelson Mandela
Metaphors We Live By by George Lakoff and Mark Johnson
Reagan: A Life in Letters by Ronald Reagan
The Autobiography of Benjamin Franklin by Benjamin Franklin
The Checklist Manifesto: How to Get Things Right by Atul Gawande
The Hero with a Thousand Faces by Joseph Campbell
The New British Constitution by Vernon Bogdanor
The Power of Myth by Joseph Campbell with Bill Moyers
Vor 1914: Erinnerungen an Frankfurt geschrieben in Israel by Selmar Spier
Walden: or, Life in the Woods by Henry David Thoreau
Why America Is Not a New Rome by Vaclav Smil

Philosophy and Theology

A Theory of Justice by John Rawls
Anarchy, the State, and Utopia by Robert Nozick
Destination Torah: Reflections on the Weekly Torah Readings by Isaac Sassoon
Halakhic Man by Joseph Soloveitchik
Letters from a Stoic by Lucius Annaeus Seneca
Man's Search for Meaning by Viktor Frankl
Meditations by Marcus Aurelius
Pirke Avot: A Modern Commentary on Jewish Ethics by Leonard Kravits and Kerry Olitzky
Plato, not Prozac! Applying Eternal Wisdom to Everyday Problems by Lou Marinoff
Tao Te Ching by Lao Tsu
The Art of War by Sun Tzu
The Consolations of Philosophy by Alain de Botton
The Mahabharata
The Power Tactics of Jesus Christ and Other Essays by Jay Haley
The Talmud

Psychology

Affect Dysregulation and Disorders of the Self by Allan Schore
Affect Regulation and the Repair of the Self by Allan Schore
Attachment and Loss by John Bowlby
Deep Survival: Who Lives, Who Dies, and Why; True Stories of Miraculous Endurance and Sudden Death by Laurence Gonzales
Descartes' Error: Emotion, Reason, and the Human Brain by Antonio Damasio
Driven to Distraction: Recognizing and Coping with Attention Deficit Disorder from Childhood through Adulthood by Edward Hallowell and John Ratey
EMDR: The Breakthrough Eye Movement Therapy for Overcoming Anxiety, Stress, and Trauma by Francine Shapiro
Flow: The Psychology of Optimal Experience by Mihaly Csikszentmihalyi
Gut Feelings: The Intelligence of the Unconscious by Gerd Gigerenzer
Influence: The Psychology of Persuasion by Robert Cialdini
Love, Medicine & Miracles: Lessons Learned about Self-Healing from a Surgeon's Experience with Exceptional Patients by Bernie Siegel
Power vs. Force: The Hidden Determinants of Human Behavior by David Hawkins
Simple Heuristics That Make Us Smart by Gerd Gigerenzer and Peter Todd
The Archaeology of Mind: Neuroevolutionary Origins of Human Emotions by Jaak Panksepp and Lucy Biven

The Art of Thinking Clearly by Rolf Dobelli

The Developing Mind: How Relationships and the Brain Interact to Shape Who We Are by Daniel Siegel

The Feeling of What Happens: Body and Emotion in the Making of Consciousness by Antonio Damasio

The 48 Laws of Power by Robert Greene

The Neuroscience of Psychotherapy: Healing the Social Brain by Louis Cozolino

There Are No Accidents: Synchronicity and the Stories of Our Lives by Robert Hopcke

Thinking, Fast and Slow by Daniel Kahneman

Waking the Tiger: Healing Trauma by Peter Levine with Ann Frederick

Willpower: Rediscovering the Greatest Human Strength by Roy Baumeister and John Tierney

Science

At Home in the Universe: The Search for the Laws of Self-Organization and Complexity by Stuart Kauffman

Connected: The Surprising Power of Our Social Networks and How They Shape Our Lives by Nicholas Christakis and James Fowler

Deep Simplicity: Bringing Order to Chaos and Complexity by John Gribbin

Emergence: The Connected Lives of Ants, Brains, Cities, and Software by Steven Johnson

How Nature Works: The Science of Self-Organized Criticality by Per Bak

Journey to the Ants: A Story of Scientific Exploration by Bert Hölldobler and Edward O. Wilson

Linked: How Everything Is Connected to Everything Else and What It Means for Business, Science, and Everyday Life by Albert-László Barabási

Phantoms in the Brain: Probing the Mysteries of the Human Mind by V. S. Ramachandran and Sandra Blakeslee

Signs of Life: How Complexity Pervades Biology by Ricard Solé and Brian Goodwin

Synaptic Self: How Our Brains Become Who We Are by Joseph LeDoux

Self-help

A Message to Garcia by Elbert Hubbard

A Simple Act of Gratitude: How Learning to Say Thank You Changed My Life by John Kralik

Acres of Diamonds by Russell Conwell

As a Man Thinketh by James Allen

Daring Greatly: How the Courage to Be Vulnerable Transforms the Way We Live, Love, Parent, and Lead by Brené Brown

Focusing by Eugene Gendlin

Getting the Love You Want: A Guide for Couples by Harville Hendrix

Getting Things Done: The Art of Stress-Free Productivity by David Allen

How to Win Friends and Influence People by Dale Carnegie

How Will You Measure Your Life? by Clayton Christensen, James Allworth, and Karen Dillon

Keeping the Love You Find: A Personal Guide by Harville Hendrix

Manifest Your Destiny: The Nine Spiritual Principles for Getting Everything You Want by Wayne Dyer

Success: Advice for Achieving Your Goals from Remarkably Accomplished People by Jena Pincott

Thanks!: How Practicing Gratitude Can Make You Happier by Robert A. Emmons

The Go-Getter: A Story That Tells You How to Be One by Peter Kyne

The Laws of Lifetime Growth: Always Make Your Future Bigger Than Your Past by Dan Sullivan and Catherine Nomura

The Power of Positive Thinking by Norman Vincent Peale

The Power of Vulnerability: Teachings on Authenticity, Connection, and Courage by Brené Brown

The Road Less Traveled: A New Psychology of Love, Traditional Values and Spiritual Growth by M. Scott Peck

Think and Grow Rich by Napoleon Hill

Thrift and Generosity: The Joy of Giving by John Templeton Jr.

INDEX